PARTIES
THAT
WOW

PARTIES
THAT
WOW

Setting the Stage for
Creative Entertaining

JONATHAN FONG

Watson-Guptill Publications
New York

The author and the publisher have made every effort to make sure that the information presented in this book is complete and accurate. Neither the author nor the publisher shall be held responsible for any loss, injury, or damage allegedly occurring from any information or advice in this book.

Senior Acquisitions Editor/Crafts: Joy Aquilino
Editor: John A. Foster
Designer: Pooja Bakri/Bakri Design
Production Director: Alyn Evans

First published in 2007 by Watson-Guptill Publications,
Crown Publishing Group,
a division of Random House Inc., New York
www.crownpublishing.com
www.watsonguptill.com

Photographs by Jessica Boone

Stamps:
Small Flower: Copyright © Magenta
Dragonfly, Butterfly with Ferns: Copyright © Hero Arts, 2006. All rights reserved
"House of Lotus Collection": Copyright © Oxford Impressions, 2001
Round Lantern, Small: Copyright © A Stamp in the Hand Co., by artist Sue Nan Douglass
Asian Image, Woman with Hat: Copyright © Inkadinkado
Wisteria, Butterfly, Hanabishi: Copyright © Mari & Me
Bird with Flower: Copyright © Viva Las Vegastamps! Used with permission
"Time for Tea": Copyright © Simply Stamped
Floral Background: Copyright © Savvy Stamps
"Celebrate," "Life": Copyright © Rubberstamp Ave.

Artists:
Invitation on page 26 by Charmaine Fuglsby, Joanne Gordon, Laura Kanno, Ellie Shaw, Teresa Stafford
Invitation on page 52 by Jessica J. Hollowell, paper artist, Los Angeles, CA
Hand-painted plate pictured on pages 52 and 56 courtesy of Cirsten Weldon
Invitation on page 90 by Charmaine Fuglsby, Joanne Gordon, Laura Kanno, Ellie Shaw, Teresa Stafford

Library of Congress Cataloging-in-Publication Data
Fong, Jonathan.
Parties that Wow / Jonathan Fong.
p. cm.
Includes bibliographical references and index.
ISBN 978-0-8230-9978-8 (alk. paper)
1. Party decorations. 2. Entertaining. 3. Parties. I. Title.
TT900.P3F65 2007
745.594'1—dc22
2007013831

Printed in China

First printing, 2007
2 3 4 5 6 7 / 13 12 11 10 09

Acknowledgments

As I say in the following pages, throwing a party is like staging a show. In that spirit, I'd like to put on a Broadway show to thank everyone who helped with this book.

For the big opening number, I'd thank my family at Watson-Guptill: Joy Aquilino, Victoria Craven, Amy Rhodes, Allison Devlin, Andrea Glickson, Lori Horak, Melissa Berger, and John Foster. The song would begin, "Who turns my ideas into pages? You do. Who lets me be a little outrageous? You do. Who else believed in me and preconceived we'd truly be a hit from the start? It's you, Watson G, it's you." (Watch out, Sondheim.)

Then, I'd do a tap dance routine for my wonderful collaborator and photographer Jessica Boone, who kept me on my toes and made sure we were on schedule.

Next would be an inspirational ballad for Joanne Gordon, my creative right arm, who helped bring so many of the projects in this book to life. She deserves an award for her supporting role.

Following that would be a chorus number with the talented people who were so generous to share their ideas and creativity: Natasha Earling, Laurie Faulkner, Monica Heeren, Jack Houck, Guy Miracle and Lance Castro, Kellie Zaleski, Sandi Silbert and her advertising class at LACHSA, Charla King, and the Card Club Ladies: Ellie Shaw, Charmaine Fuglsby, Teresa Stafford, Laura Kanno, and Jessica Hollowell.

Up next would be a scene in which dishes and silverware dance and sing, to honor my chef and food stylist, Amy Jurist.

Of course, there would be a dazzling production number featuring many changes of scenery to thank the people who let me photograph in their homes and backyards: Kitty Bartholomew, David Brooks and Len Greco, Stephanie Burns, Sandra Dupont and Miklos Fulop, Deborah Kautzky, and Sheri Sanders.

Then I'd choreograph a Busby Berkeley extravaganza for my agent, Deborah Warren, who pushed me on stage and said, "You're going out there an interior designer, but you're coming back an author."

An onstage water ballet would follow for Monique Raphel High, who first navigated me through the publishing seas.

And for the final number, I'd fly through the air on wires, thanking my biggest cheerleader, Greg Phillips. He helps me defy gravity.

So to all of the above, as well as the countless others out there who've given me so much support and encouragement, please take a bow.

Oh yeah, I'll be selling books in the lobby after the show.

Contents

Introduction

I'm a party animal. Well, not in the sense of getting crazy and dancing with a lampshade on my head. Actually, I don't even drink. So being a teetotaler, I have to come up with other ways to liven up a party.

For me, parties are about more than just the drinks, or the food. It's about entertaining. And I mean entertaining in the truest sense of the word. I like to give my guests a front row center seat to an experience that is theatrical, fun, and memorable. A great party is like a Broadway show, even if we're talking about a small cocktail party. Like they say in the musical *Chicago*, "Give 'em the old razzle dazzle."

I think the desire to put so much showmanship in my parties stems from my initial insecurity. In Los Angeles, there are so many things to do on the weekend, why would anyone want to come to my house for dinner? If people were going to give up their precious Saturday night, I thought I had better make it worth their while. There was also the fact that I wasn't a particularly good cook. Nor was I well versed in hoity-toity details like wine selection or silverware placement. What I could do was put on a show. So that's what I did.

But what grew out of my neurotic need to please became a lot of fun. I could not wait to throw parties because I loved the planning, the decorating, and the creativity. Since I had decorated every wall and room in my house already, the tablescape was my last frontier. And my friends loved it. They didn't seem to care that my food was from Costco. All that mattered was that they were thoroughly entertained.

In this book, I've featured eighteen of my favorite party themes. Some are based around world destinations, some around special occasions, and others are just fun themes. Please feel free to mix and match ideas from the parties. If you like the invitation from one party but want to make a centerpiece from another, by all means do so. Also, don't feel like you have to do every project presented for each party. Even just doing one little thing can be enough to wow your guests. So use this book as an inspiration sourcebook. Pick and choose ideas as you go.

Within these pages, you'll find over 100 party ideas. And unlike my previous books where I have very detailed, step-by-step instructions to complete each project, most of these ideas are so simple that the photograph and a quick description pretty much say it all. For some projects, I do list a few steps, but even they don't require much explanation. And for the party ideas that require a little more work, don't worry, I do give you a materials list and detailed instructions.

But remember: This book is not a cookbook. I don't even pretend to be a chef. Like I said, for my parties, I go to Costco or at best do takeout. Believe me, it tastes much better than anything I can whip up. What I'd rather spend my time doing is making the food look beautiful. So throughout the book I've included some ideas on presenting food, not cooking it. It's up to you whether you use pre-made food or cook from scratch with your own recipes. Presentation is still everything.

You know, there's nothing I enjoy more than having a few friends over for some food, conversation, and laughs. I don't get to see people nearly as often as I'd like, so I treasure these opportunities. When you get down to it, all the party ideas in this book are secondary to the privilege of slowing down and sharing time with the people you care about. But because these times are so precious, making the effort to stage a truly memorable affair honors your guests. It's a way of respecting them, of thanking them. And that, actually, is the secret to **Parties that Wow.**

Putting on the Show

I say that throwing a party is like putting on a show, not just because I'm a theater fan but because the analogy provides a clear planning guide for us. So how do we make sure our party is more like *Mamma Mia* than *Les Miserables*? Well, take your orchestra seat, my friend, and read on. We've got a show to do!

The Script

In the theater, it all starts with the script. With a party, it starts with selecting a theme and carrying it out. Of course, a party doesn't always have to have a theme. But choosing one gives you a framework to plan the party. It helps you with decorating, flower arrangements, and even menu selection. For example, imagine how much easier it is if you know you're having an Asian-inspired dinner. When you're shopping and planning, keep your eye out for Asian details and avoid the maracas. I don't know about you, but having the planning choices narrowed down for me really helps. I'm a Libra, so it's hard for me to make up my mind.

But don't be a slave to the theme, either. If every single detail is themed, you run the risk of having an over-the-top party that is a little bit garish. We've seen these parties on the news, and they're usually thrown by deposed CEOs who've squandered the life savings of stockholders. By all means, you can veer off the theme if you'd like. Use it as a roadmap, but make your own creative choices. If you want to serve sushi at your Parisian party, that's fine. Since you had a starting point, I see that as making a conscious decision to meld genres, rather than being aimless.

The Set

Great set design can really make or break a production. I'm all for minimalism, but I have to admit that I love it when I walk into a theater or auditorium and see that the stage has been transformed. The same goes for staging a party. When your friends step into your home, you want them to say, "Wow! Look at what you've done for the party," rather than "Did we come on the wrong day?" Remember, it's all about honoring your guests, coupled with a little effort.

For one of my holiday parties, I rented a pickup truck and drove two hours away to the mountains and filled the truck up with snow so that I could decorate my home with it. The side of the truck advertised a rental fee of $19.95 a day, but I didn't realize that the company also charged for mileage. Needless to say, it turned out to be very expensive snow. Still, what a sight all that snow was! People still talk about it, especially at U-Haul.

Obviously, I'm not asking you go to these extremes. Designing the set of your party can encompass something as simple as placing flowers on your table or turning on the porch light. This is where I come in. I'm chock-full of ideas for centerpieces, table decorations, and temporary wall treatments. You name it, I have an idea, and I'm sure that you, too, will soon discover the joy of sets.

The Effects

Once you've decided on your theme and have a handle on how the party's going to look, it's time for the special touches. From the lighting to food presentation, it's the details that matter. For example, in the theater, the lighting does more than just show the actors' faces. It defines the space, sets the mood, and drives the action. The same goes for the lighting at your party. Only light areas where you want your guests to focus. If your kitchen is preparation headquarters, keep the lights low to hide the mess. Use lighting to let people know if they should be in the living room or the dining room. The action will follow the lighting. Avoid bright lighting; you're not trying scare away roaches. When the lights are dimmed, your guests will know the performance is beginning. Also, soft lighting, especially candlelight, evens out skin tones and makes everyone look their best.

Special touches are even more important when serving food. When I worked in advertising, we relied on food stylists to make the dishes look absolutely perfect for our ads. Pay special attention when you're flipping through magazines or looking through beautifully photographed cookbooks to gather ideas for presenting your food. Some common features in exquisitely presented food are as follows:

- **Restraint** Don't pile on the grub. Negative space on the plate actually highlights the food. When there's a lot going on, people don't know where to look. That's why I like large plates, even if what I'm serving only occupies a small part of the plate's space.
- **Composition** Food presented vertically has almost become a cliché, but I agree with the basic concept that artful, creative placement of components makes a dish more appetizing. For me, plating food is a lot like decorating. Will the elements look better in a row, up or down, or side-by-side? Does the food look better centered or placed on the left? Does it look good by itself or is something missing?
- **Contrast** When everything on the plate is the same color, it looks like mush. Contrast creates visual interest and, in turn, appetite appeal. Of course, if you're talking about a bowl of mashed potatoes, it will obviously be the same color, yet a simple dash of paprika could add the perfect amount of contrast.
- **The Unexpected** Food is entertainment, and when you surprise with an unusual twist, people are wowed. Especially when it's so simple—they wonder why they didn't think of it themselves. I present some rather unorthodox ideas in the following chapters that will impress and amuse your guests.

The Cast

Everyone has a role to play at your party, either as the perfect host or as the perfect guest, and everyone has to play his or her part to ensure a successful event.

The host has the responsibility to invite the right mix of people, to finish decorating before the party starts, to ensure that everyone has enough to eat, and that everyone has a good time. As the host, you have a myriad of responsibilities. To borrow another theater metaphor, the most important thing to remember is that as the host, you are the lead actor, and you must allow the other cast members, the guests, to shine. Remember, the party is not about you; it's about them.

Now a little word to the guests, which, at one point or another, we all are. When a host puts the effort into throwing a party, guests should follow a few common courtesies, listed below:

- Make sure to RSVP.
- Unless it's an open house, arrive at the appointed hour.
- Don't bring an additional guest without asking the host first, and limit the number to one.
- Bring a small gift of appreciation, but don't expect the host to open it then and there.
- If you have food allergies or aversions, let the host know at least a week in advance, instead of the night before. Your host has shopping to do.
- Don't make out with your date. It makes everyone uncomfortable.
- Don't ask the host if you can watch the big game.
- Meet other guests. They are just as shy as you and will love you forever for initiating a conversation.
- Send a thank-you note, even if it's via e-mail. If you've taken any photos, attach one. Your host will appreciate it.

There. I think that about covers it. Now it's time to turn the page and have some fun!

PART 1

WORLD TOURS

The best parties have an escapist quality to them. They're 180 degrees from everyday life. So why not escape with your guests to another part of the world? Figuratively speaking, of course. Parties themed with world destinations are rich in possibilities, both in decor and food. And, you can get a taste of another country without getting jet lag or dealing with other tourists. In this section, I've included parties based on places that many people have visited, like Paris, and some that no one ever will, like ancient Egypt—unless you have a time machine. If parties are like shows, then these are sweeping epics. Be careful, though: Your guests may not want to go home.

CHAPTER I

Bon Soirée

Capturing the Charm of a Paris Flea Market

J'adore Paris. Ah, how I love the sidewalk cafes, the Eiffel Tower, the glorious food, and the people-watching. And that's just at Paris, Las Vegas. When I finally visited the actual City of Lights, I felt like my heart had found its home. The history and architecture were awe inspiring. Everyone seemed to be so chic and attractive. And any remnant of a carb-free diet went out the window when I bit into those impossibly crunchy yet chewy-soft baguettes . . . yum-mee.

This Paris flea market party is truly one of my favorites. It has an effortless flair that captures the adventures I had walking along the streets of Paris. Because of its quirky charm, I feel like it's a get-together that the movie character Amelie would throw. Many people are afraid of hosting parties because they don't know how to coordinate place settings or how to properly place glassware. This party's perfect, because nothing matches and anything goes, except for berets and maybe mimes—they can stay across the Atlantic.

French Postcards

I know in this age of e-mail, people rarely get good, old-fashioned party invitations anymore. I do enjoy the convenience of electronic invites, especially as they make RSVPs so much easier, but when you send a real invitation, it will start some buzz. Every party in this book comes with an invitation idea, some being more elaborate than others. They're here to inspire, so use the ideas as you wish.

A vintage postcard saying, "Wish you were here" is a natural invitation for this Paris party. I bought a stack of French postcards from eBay for less than $5. Almost all of them had writing and authentic French postmarks and stamps, giving them a historic bent. Include a few of these postcards with a blank one that has your invitation written on it. If you can't find a blank one, scan a postcard and use a computer graphics program like Photoshop to erase the writing. Your guests will feel like you're sending them an invitation from another place, and another time.

Picture Frame Place Settings

When I go to flea markets, I can't pass up picture frames. Sometimes, I'll even buy a framed painting, toss the artwork, and keep the frame. I look for a weathered patina, one suggesting a rich history, or maybe even a brush with the *Mona Lisa*. And as you can see, they look *tres chic* on the table. I've mismatched dinner and salad plates, silverware, and glasses and placed them inside the frames, so each place setting looks like a whimsical work of art. Look for frames with an 11- x 14-inch opening, which is the perfect size to fit a standard 11-inch plate.

Sparkling Vases

At my local deli, they carry imported sparkling French lemonade. After drinking the lemonade, I keep the vintage-looking bottles with swing tops. They make perfect vases for wildflowers. It's as if you were saying, "I've been shopping on the Left Bank all day and just had time to throw these arrangements together." They're adorable, yet they look very spontaneous.

Louvre Stands

On my table, I like to display things at different heights. It not only makes the table more dynamic, it improves sight lines so nothing gets lost. So raise the flowers, or even the salt and pepper shakers, to another level. You'll help them stand out.

These stands feature famous paintings, like the *Mona Lisa*, decoupaged onto wood blocks. They're works of art in and of themselves.

WHAT YOU'LL NEED FOR ONE STAND
5 reprints of paintings
Wood block, sanded smooth
Bowl of water
White glue
Foam brushes
Rubber brayer
Acrylic polyurethane
1 tin can (optional)

1   Cut the reprints to fit the sides of the block. I recommend covering five sides of the block and leaving the bottom side blank.

2   Dip the artwork in water to relax the paper. In the meantime, paint a layer of white glue onto the wood with a foam brush.

3   Place the wet reprint onto the wood. Because the paper is wet, the reprint will be easy to move around. Roll a rubber brayer on top of the artwork to remove any excess water and glue. Repeat for all five sides. Let dry overnight.

4   Apply three coats of acrylic polyurethane to each side with a foam brush. I place the block on a can so that I can apply the polyurethane without it sticking to the table.

Pomme Frites

Authentically, french fries aren't French, but they're not American, either. They're the national snack of Belgium, where you'll find them served in paper cones. I've added a Parisian touch by wrapping these french fries in French fashion ads.

Party Tip

An amusing touch for when your guests powder their noses is to play French language CDs in the bathroom, which you can borrow from the public library.

High-Heeled Napkin Holders

These shoes are so *Moulin Rouge*. They remind me of those foreign movies in which flirtatious men drink out of women's shoes. That always grossed me out, but I guess it's supposed to be romantic. Anyway, these shoes make sassy holders for your cocktail napkins. Of course, they've never been worn.

Sofa Makeover

If your living room doesn't have the look of a Paris flea market, here's an easy way to transform your sofa and give it a new look. I first did this sofa re-do for a home makeover television show. We called it "CPR": Couch-Pillow Resuscitation. It's also a great way to temporarily cover your furniture to protect it from clumsy guests, and it looks so good you may actually want to keep your sofa this way.

1 Find a queen-size duvet cover with a fabulous print. I prefer duvet covers to actual slipcovers, because the patterns and styles are much more interesting.

2 Place your sofa cushions inside the duvet cover and button it up.

3 Return the cushions, now wrapped in the duvet, and tuck in the excess fabric.

4 Decorate the sofa with various throws and pillows.

CHAPTER 2

Zen Fusion

Celebrating the Classic Simplicity of the Far East

There is a dichotomy to Asian design. On one end of the spectrum, there's the grand opulence associated with imperial China, a look we know well from martial arts epics and old-fashioned Chinese restaurants. The color palette is cinnabar red, royal gold, and jade green, and the style is awash in flowing silks, shimmering velvets, and ornate embroidery. I love this particular design because it's so theatrical.

On the opposite end of the Asian design spectrum, there's Zen. It is a philosophy of restraint and harmony. The color palette is neutral, with shades of slate, putty, and stone. Interiors are streamlined and orderly, incorporating natural materials like wood and pebbles. The look is simple, elegant, and quiet. The party I've designed for this chapter leans more toward Zen. It's a versatile look for a variety of entertaining occasions, because the style transcends its Asian origins. The clean lines and simple details are universal. It just goes to show, the Far East doesn't have to be so far out.

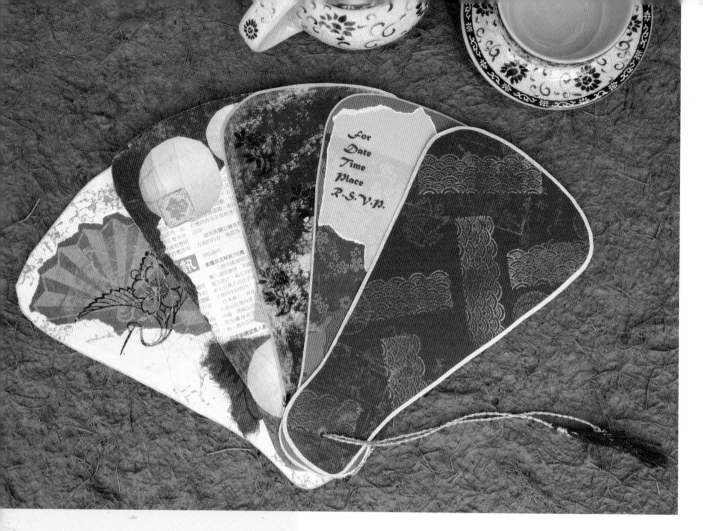

Fan Invitation

I asked the Card Club Ladies, a very talented group of artists, to help me design some invitations for this book, and I am honored to include their creations. For this Zen party, they designed a fan invitation that is not only lovely but also deceptively simple to make.

1. Cut a fan blade with card stock (you can even use a file folder), and punch a hole on the bottom. The shape should be a form of a triangle, but it's up to you whether to make it curved or angular. Use the first fan blade as a template to make the others. Attaching several blades together makes a more impressive invitation; therefore, I used five, but your invitation can consist of just one blade, if you like.

2. Decorate each blade with paint, paper, stamps, and ephemera. On one of the blades, include the party details.

3. Attach the fan blades together with a ribbon or tassel.

Hot Sesame

Sesame is one of my favorite aromas. In fact, at my parent's Chinese restaurant, one of their cooking secrets was to drizzle some sesame oil over the entrées right before they were served. In this project, sesame seeds form a fragrant bed on which to lay a votive candle. Gracing each place setting, the sesame votive welcomes guests with style.

Sticks and Stones

In Asian culture, one never lays chopsticks flat on the table. I'm not sure if it's a matter of etiquette or hygiene, or maybe both. The next time you go to a Chinese or Japanese restaurant, notice how some people fold up the paper chopstick sleeve and then place the chopsticks on it. At Asian stores, they sell chopstick rests, but a simple polished stone does the trick even more beautifully.

The Great Wall

A room divider is a practical way to section off your dining area, thereby defining the space and creating a mini sanctuary for your party. This bamboo divider can be constructed in minutes, and you just might decide to leave it up permanently.

1 Place the dry floral foam in the metal bin so that they are snug. I used two bins for this divider because they were so small.

2 Push the six-foot bamboo poles into the floral foam so that they are lined up in a row. In my divider, I used six poles per metal bin.

3 Insert a three-foot bamboo pole into the floral foam at an angle. Tie the diagonal three-foot pole to each six-foot pole at the spot where they meet with raffia. This will stabilize the bamboo. Finally, cover the floral foam with sheet moss and rocks.

Year of the Horsetail

In the spirit of Zen, this lovely floral arrangement is so minimalist that it doesn't even have a vase. That's because horsetail and orchids are very hearty and thrive for days without water.

1. Cut horsetails to approximately ten-inch lengths. The horsetail stalks pictured came very long, but you can usually get about three pieces per stalk.

2. Tie the horsetail together with raffia so that the diameter of the bunch is about five inches.

3. Slide a stem of orchids underneath the raffia to add vibrant color to the centerpiece.

On the Rocks

The presentation of these store-bought chicken skewers is stunning, as the black rocks set off the color of the appetizers. The organic backdrop is unexpected, and so much cooler than a doily.

1 Wash rocks with dish soap, rinse, and dry.

2 Place rocks in a platter.

3 Set chicken skewers on the rocks.

Note

You can also warm the rocks by placing them in the oven on "warm." Don't heat the rocks, because rocks can explode when too hot.

The same concept can work with large Chinese black beans instead of rocks. Here, shrimp tempura rests on the beans so elegantly that no one would ever know that you bought the shrimp at Costco.

Party Tip

Give your bathroom a little makeover when you have a party. Place some river rocks in the sink, light a scented candle, and change the light bulbs to colored lights. If you have a bathtub, fill it with water and float candles and flowers in it.

CHAPTER 3

One Night in Morocco

A Restaurant Patio Is Transformed into Casablanca

When I think of Morocco, my imagination goes into overdrive. There's the exotic lure of sun-drenched bazaars; the dizzying fragrance of spices, piled high in earthenware; and veiled beauties dancing in the blue moonlight. But most exciting of all is the sense of danger and intrigue. Forbidden liaisons. Bogey and Bacall. And secret messages hidden under my fez hat.

With imagery this evocative (and downright cinematic), I was thrilled that my friend Laurie Faulkner was planning on throwing a Moroccan-themed party at a local restaurant. Now, this restaurant is an American bar and grill, with no hint of Moroccan flair whatsoever. Our challenge, then, was to turn a plain outdoor patio into a scintillating den of exoticism. If you're planning an event at a restaurant rather than your own home, this chapter also affords some valuable lessons in working with an outside venue. With clear communication and cooperation, your party will run smoothly—and you don't have to wash the dishes.

So be prepared to be swept away. And here's looking at you, kid.

You Are Invited to

One Night In Morocco

The indigo night is warm,
and the air fragrant with spices.
Succumb to an evening of Moroccan mystique.
Saturday, May 6th
7:30 ... 1:30 pm

Scroll Invitation

This beaded scroll instantly transports your invitees to a faraway land. It unfolds to reveal a pocket, which carries the details of the party. There's pageantry to this invitation that I just love. People will have no choice but to RSVP "yes," with bangles on.

WHAT YOU'LL NEED

2 wooden doll pins
Masking tape
Scissors
1 sheet of decorative paper
   with a rough fiber texture
   (approx. 12 x 20 inches)
White all-purpose glue
1 yard of beaded trim
1 glue-on embellishment
1 tassel
1 paper invitation

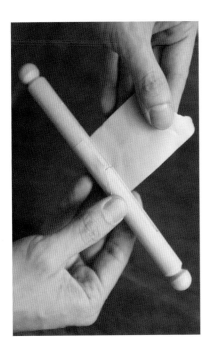

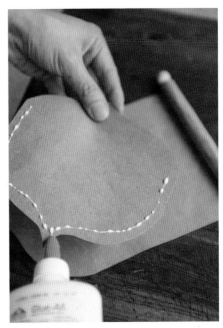

1   To make the arm of the scroll, place two wooden doll pins end to end and tape the two pins together with masking tape.

2   Cut a piece of decorative paper that's about six inches wide by twelve inches long. Wrap the six-inch side around the doll pins and glue the paper around the pins.

3   Next, cut a smaller piece of paper that's about six inches by six inches, with the top and bottom curved, as shown in the photo. Trim the bottom of the longer piece of paper so that it matches up with the bottom of the smaller piece. Then glue the two pieces together, leaving the top open for the pocket.

4   Glue the beaded trim to the edge of the entire scroll. Add an embellishment to the pocket, and finish it off by tying a tassel to the bottom. Finally, slip the paper invitation into the pocket.

Fabric Tent

More than anything else, the flowing fabric canopy is what gives this room a Moroccan flavor. The fabric envelops the room in rich colors, while also hiding the unattractive lattice ceiling. We bought the fabric for $1 a yard in Los Angeles's Little India (they're actually saris), but any sheer fabric will do. It's just like putting up streamers—that easy!

1 Starting at the edge of the room, attach the fabric to the wall with pushpins or small nails.

2 Take the length of the fabric to the middle of the room and attach it to the ceiling with pushpins or nails, or tie it to the light fixture, if there is one.

Spice Trays

Small plates of fennel are great to have on tables. Not only are the seeds intensely fragrant, but they also act as after-dinner breath mints. Pour some seeds into a shallow bowl or tray, and then garnish it with some fresh orchids. Don't worry; orchids stay fresh out of water for hours, so these spice trays will continue to look beautiful until the wee hours—just like you.

Mirror Centerpiece

For a centerpiece dripping with atmosphere, here's an idea that's easy to put together, but has that "Wow!" visual impact. Start with a Moroccan mirror. Place a small lantern, a few votive candles, and some beads and gold coins on it. For added detail, glue some beaded trim around the rim of the glass votives. And yes, that's a toy snake lurking at the edge. It gives the centerpiece an element of danger, as if Mata Hari has discovered that you're a double agent and needs to silence you—I guess I've seen too many Saturday afternoon movies.

Topiary Garland

Shimmering garlands decorated with lush topiaries hang at the patio's entrance, beckoning guests to partake of the pleasures within. These garlands can also act as a room divider or as a backdrop to a gift table.

WHAT YOU'LL NEED FOR ONE TOPIARY
(Each garland has two topiaries)
1 piece of 3 x 12-inch chicken wire
Wire cutters
12 feet (approx.) of floral mesh
Hook or nail
1 piece of floral foam
Red and yellow flowers, such as dahlias and protea
1 fern leaf
2 yards of beaded ribbon

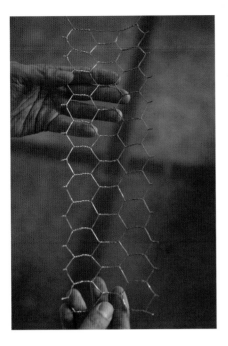

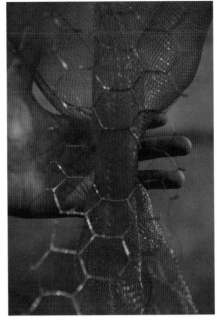

1 Buy a roll of chicken wire that's twelve inches wide. Using wire cutters, cut a small piece so that there are three hexagons across, with little or no extra wires on the sides except on the top. These long wires on top will come in handy later.

2 Cut a length of floral mesh that's a little more than the height of the ceiling. (Floral mesh comes in rolls of about thirty feet.) Hook or nail one end of the mesh to the ceiling and let it hang. Thread the mesh through one of the middle holes of the chicken wire and out from another hole, as shown in the photograph above.

3 Place a small piece of wet floral foam in the middle of the chicken wire and wrap the ends of the chicken wire around the foam. Use the long wires from Step 1 to keep the wire secure.

4 Now insert the flowers and fern leaf around the foam. You will have room for two topiaries per length of floral mesh, but just one is fine if you run out of time. Finally, add a strand of beaded ribbon around one of the topiaries for a sparkling touch.

Cinnamon Floral Garnish

When you're having a party at a restaurant, you don't have a lot of say in how the food will be presented. Typically, if waiters are passing hors d'oeuvres, the food will be on trays with paper doilies. You can ask the restaurant management if you can add a small garnish to the trays, however. It's these little details that make all the difference.

To go along with the spice theme, I chose to make cinnamon garnishes. The great thing about a cinnamon stick is that it has a natural opening that you can slide floral stems into. Tie a couple of these cinnamon-encased flowers together and you have a tasty garnish.

Incense Favors

Let your guests take home a fragrant reminder of the evening. You can find boxes of incense at many import gift stores or Middle Eastern markets. (And by Middle Eastern, I don't mean Ohio.) Wrap them in cellophane with ribbon and place all the favors in a large chest. It's the perfect ending to a perfect party.

Party Tip

If you're asking a friend to take pictures at your party, provide a shot list of what you want photographed. Otherwise, you might end up with photos of just your friend's date.

HELPFUL HINTS WHEN HAVING A PARTY AT A RESTAURANT

- Find out what the management will let you do in terms of decorating the venue. Be specific about what you plan to do, and have it approved in writing.

- Obtain as much time as possible from the restaurant to set up. Make sure you will have access to the venue so that you and your crew can work without disrupting the restaurant's normal operations. Have this time confirmed in your written contract.

- See if you can remove the decorations the next day instead of immediately after the party. The last thing you want to do at the end of a long evening is to clean up. Again, have the time frame in writing.

- Keep track of the tab. Many restaurants will charge you for a minimum drink guarantee. For example, the restaurant may charge you $1,000 for a minimum drink fee, which means they're counting on your guests to spend at least $1,000 on drinks. If the bar bill comes up short of that amount, you are responsible for the difference. You must be diligent in seeing that every time your guests purchase a drink, it is credited to your account. With other customers in the restaurant sharing the bar, the bartender might not know which people are your guests. You could offer drink vouchers, but that's a pain. Instead, ask your guests to remind the bartender that they are in your party. Place a small sign on the bar to remind guests, and periodically check that the bartender is keeping an accurate tab.

CHAPTER 4

Rock Like an Egyptian

A Party Fit for Cleopatra

I think I may have been Cleopatra in a former life. I like having hired help, I don't like snakes, and I have always been fascinated by Egypt. When I was in eighth grade, I was obsessed by the supposed mystical powers of pyramids, and for my Mentally Gifted Minors project, I conducted an experiment in which I placed a plant under a pyramid to see if it grew faster than a plant that was not under a pyramid. (The results were inconclusive, as I only watered the plant that was under the pyramid.) I even wanted to sleep under a pyramid, because I thought it would give me eternal youth. Of course, now I know you just need a good moisturizer.

I haven't been back to Egypt since my reign there, so this party brings me back to the old days. But seriously, an Egyptian-themed party is such fun, because it revisits the fantasy cinematic terrain that we know so well from the *Mummy* movies, *Indiana Jones*, and even *The Three Stooges*. So whether you're a reincarnated pharaoh or not, you'll have a blast. And if you don't, well, you're just in de-Nile.

IT'S
AN
EGYPTIAN
PARTY

Ancient Papyrus

Nothing says "Come to Mummy" like an ancient scroll invitation encrypted with Egyptian hieroglyphics. I used to think that hieroglyphics were just random symbols that you could make up, but it is an actual alphabet. Hieroglyphics are a phonetic alphabet, so not every letter in our alphabet has a corresponding symbol. Consult the chart at right to write your own messages. Just select the hieroglyphs that have the closest matching sound for your word. For example, the sound "b," signified by the hieroglyph of the foot, would cover our letters *b* and *v* because the sounds are similar.

1 Tear the edges of a piece of parchment or marbleized paper.

2 Write your invitation in hieroglyphics.

3 Roll it up and place it in a box.

4 Add some sand and a few pebbles.

5 If you're not going to write the translation directly on the invitation, be sure to include a hieroglyphic alphabet in the box so your guests can decode the message.

Sound/Letter	Hieroglyph	Sound/Letter	Hieroglyph
short A		H	
long A/Ah		J	
B		M	
soft C/S		N	
hard C		P	
D		R	
E/I		T	
F		W	
G		Y/EE	

Hieroglyphics by Sandi Silbert

Light Pyramid

You can't have an Egyptian party without a pyramid. I chose to create a pyramid above the bar, because the structure is supposed to prolong life. So why not make the liquor last longer?

WHAT YOU'LL NEED
Small, square table
1 tall, skinny object at least thirty
    inches high (I used a plant
    stand from T.J. Maxx)
1 strand of 100 miniature lights
Electrical tape

1 Place the tall, skinny object in the middle of the table.

2 One strand of 100 miniature lights made the pyramid pictured. Using electrical tape, tape one end of the lights to the top of the object you're using. Then bring the strand of lights to the corner of the table and tape the lights at the corner. Pull the lights taut so that they don't sag.

3 Bring the lights along the edge of the table to the adjacent corner and tape the lights. Then pull the lights up to the top of the tall object, again taping at the top, thereby creating a triangle.

4 Repeat, making the lighted triangle on the opposite side of the table. Notice that you are forming two triangles to create the pyramid effect. At right is a diagram of a top-down view of the pyramid for you to see the path and direction of the lights.

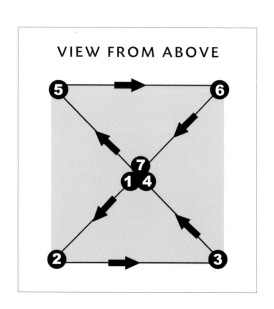

VIEW FROM ABOVE

Cleopatra's Barge

Turn your sofa into a barge on the Nile for your guests to lounge and luxuriate. Fanning your guests with palm fronds is optional.

1 Tuck bamboo poles in each corner of the sofa. Wedge the poles between the cushions and the sofa frame to keep them steady. Notice that I've used the same bamboo poles that were in The Great Wall project on page 28. Recycle those party props!

2 Drape fabric over the poles to create a canopy.

3 Peel grapes and eat.

Hieroglyphic Platters

These stone tiles look like they fell off the Great Pyramid, and they're great for serving your party food. They're also inexpensive enough for each guest to have his or her own platter, personalized with his or her name in hieroglyphics. In the photo, I spelled out "Jonathan."

1 Purchase porcelain floor tiles at your local home improvement store; they're about a dollar each. Wash and dry them before using.

2 Using the hieroglyphic alphabet on page 45, write your name, friends' names, or anything you'd like on the platters. I searched high and low for the right paint to use that would not harm if ingested, and the best medium turns out to be Betty Crocker Drizzlers. Just microwave the pouch of chocolate frosting and squeeze out the chocolate onto the platter. The tip is narrow enough so that you can write with it. The chocolate then hardens at room temperature, allowing your hieroglyphics to stay in place.

Food Pyramid

1 Spray the inside of the mold with a vegetable oil release spray.

2 Spoon three flavors of hummus into the mold to create three layers. You may need to freeze the hummus for a few minutes so that it holds its shape.

Pyramids are said to hold hidden treasures of the pharaohs. This one holds delicious layers of hummus from Trader Joe's. It's easy to create with the help of a metal pyramid mold from a gourmet food supply store.

3 Invert the mold onto your platter and gently separate the mold from the hummus pyramid.

Yummy Mummies

Send a mummy home with your guests. These party favors are Snickers chocolate bars wrapped in gauze. To give it the proportions of a human body, be sure to build up a larger layer of gauze about a third of the way down the length of the chocolate bar, where the chest and crossed arms would be.

Party Tip

Circulate a guest book throughout the evening so that everyone can write a message in it. As a host, the party can be such a blur that you might not even remember was there. The guest book is an enjoyable way to relive the party immediately that night, or years later.

JANE
AUSTEN

PRIDE A
PREJUDI

EVERYMAN'S LIBRAR

CHAPTER 5

A Jane Austen Picnic

A Genteel Afternoon of Tea and Sandwiches

The world that Jane Austen paints in her novels is sure a civilized one. Everyone calls each other Mister and Miss so-and-so. Everyone knows how to dance. And best of all, no one ever seems to work. All they do is read, knit, and play matchmaker. How idyllic is that? In fashioning this Jane Austen picnic, I wanted to create the same carefree, lazy afternoon that is so rare in the twenty-first century. I don't know about you, but I always feel like there's something I should be doing. If I haven't checked my e-mail in the last fifteen minutes, I'm afraid I've missed something. So a party that is a throwback to a less complicated era sounds like bliss.

Besides the simple pleasures that this party promises, I'm also drawn to the country cottage style of the period. I may be known for my modern, pop art design aesthetic, but the shabby chic look of tea roses, antique plates, and worn books is, surprisingly, a welcome respite for me. Yes, I do enjoy venturing into the land of frou-frou every now and then, but only for an afternoon—I have to return some text messages!

A Novel Invitation

For an invitation to a Jane Austen picnic, I thought an altered book would be ideal. But creating altered books is a meticulous craft, one that I can't explain in a few paragraphs. So I asked the talented paper artist Jessica Hollowell, whose work has been featured in the paper arts magazine *Somerset Studio,* how to make a simplified version. When she presented me with this invitation, an altered version of Jane Austen's *Pride and Prejudice,* I was in awe. Jessica has streamlined the process by altering only two pages, with the actual invitation coming out of an envelope on the page. Although it looks like there are a lot of steps involved, it really depends on how elaborate you want your invitation to be. Your version can be simpler, or even more embellished if you want the creative challenge.

WHAT YOU'LL NEED FOR ONE INVITATION

1 copy of *Pride and Prejudice*
Glue stick
Bone folder
Acrylic paint
Foam brush
Decorative papers
Coin envelope
Oval punch, or scissors
Distress Ink (optional)
Paper flowers
Card stock
Ribbon

1. Tear out the following paragraph from Chapter 28 of *Pride and Prejudice,* which is perfect for this occasion, and save it for later:

> "I confess," said he, "that I should not have been at all surprised by her ladyship's asking us on Sunday to drink tea and spend the evening at Rosings. I rather expected, from my knowledge of her affability, that it would happen. But who could have foreseen such an attention as this? Who could have imagined that we should receive an invitation to dine there (an invitation, moreover, including the whole party) so immediately after your arrival!"

2. Choosing a place in the middle of the book, glue two pages together with a glue stick. Then glue the next two pages together, so that you have two double-thick pages facing each other.

3. Smooth the pages with a bone folder, a tool that's used to flatten paper. Allow to dry completely.

4. Paint the glued pages with a few coats of acrylic paint using a foam brush. You will still be able to see the writing through the paint. In the altered book pictured opposite, *Lumiere Pearl Turquoise* by Jacquard was used. Let the paint dry thoroughly, and don't close the book, or the pages will stick together.

5. Cut decorative papers of your choice and glue them onto these pages. Pictured in the photo are some of the ones used in this invitation. Try to use a couple of different patterns so that you can overlap them.

6. On the right page, there is an envelope that holds the invitation. Find a large coin envelope, like the one shown, and cut it open to use as a template. With the template, make your own envelope with the paper of your choice. Cut the top off the envelope and oval punch it halfway. (If you don't have an oval punch, cut a semicircle with scissors.)

7. Glue your envelope on the right page at an angle. Layer torn decorative paper on top of the envelope. If you ink around the edges of the envelope, you'll create shadows and depth.

8. Now glue the torn paragraph from Step 1 on top. If you wish, put an antique finish on the quote with Distress Ink (aged mahogany is shown).

9. Embellish the envelope with paper flowers.

10. Cut a piece of card stock for the actual invitation, punch a hole at the top, and thread ribbon through the hole. Write the invitation details on the card.

11. On the left page, you'll notice a little note flap. To make it, cut a colored piece of card stock, fold, and glue onto the page. Add more layers of decorative paper and paper flowers on top. You can also stamp or write an additional message on the inside of the note.

1. Photograph various plates, pointing the camera down on them. I photographed them against a white backdrop so that the plates would stand out.

2. Using a computer graphics program, size the plates to approximately 8½ inches, so that the image will fit on an 8½- x 11-inch sheet of paper.

3. Print the plate images with your home inkjet printer onto transfer paper. I used Avery's Dark T-Shirt Transfers. Even if your cloth is light-colored, I still recommend the transfers for dark shirts, because the image will be opaque and not allow the color of the cloth to bleed through.

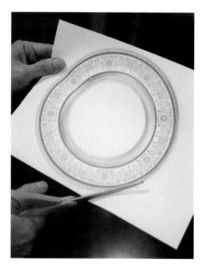

4. Cut the plate out of the transfer and iron onto your cloth, following the package instructions. Place the images randomly around the edge of the tablecloth.

Trompe l'Oeil Tablecloth

We're used to seeing trompe l'oeil on walls, but this is the first time I've seen it on a tablecloth. This delightful table covering features photo-realistic plates scattered all over. The faux plates look so realistic, because they are photographs that have been ironed onto the cloth. Can you tell which are the real plates and which are the facsimiles?

Weathered Page Vase

Just a part of a page from *Pride and Prejudice* turns this ordinary rectangular glass vase into a literary masterpiece. The image is applied to the vase with Lazertran decal paper, which is so much fun to play with. Basically, you wet the paper and slide the image onto the vase and then fill the vase with flowers. It's really hard to make a mistake.

1. Scan the page of your choice from *Pride and Prejudice,* or any novel.

2. Using a computer graphics program, size the page to fit the vase. I enlarged the page for a bolder look.

3. Print the page onto the Lazertran waterslide decal paper and trim it to fit the vase.

4. Soak the paper in water for about a minute. The decal will begin to slide off the backing paper.

5. Slide the decal onto the vase. It will be wet and very easy to position. Use your fingers to remove air bubbles and excess moisture. When the decal is wet, it is transparent, but as it dries it will become opaque.

6. To remove the image after your party, just run the vase under water until the decal slides off. If you would like to keep the image on your vase permanently, seal it with a layer of polyurethane. Water-based polyurethane will leave the image opaque; oil-based polyurethane will make it transparent.

Ribbon-Laced Basket

Turn an ordinary picnic basket into a breath of fresh spring air with the simple addition of ribbons and flowers. The decoration adds so much to the presentation. Another thing I've done with picnic baskets is to tie a large ribbon around the entire basket and top it off with a bow. When it's time to eat, I cut the ribbon, as if opening a present.

1 A picnic basket has small gaps where the strips of wood have been woven. Thread thin pieces of ribbon through the gaps. Allow about six inches of ribbon on either side to tie a bow with.

2 Cut a flower, leaving a couple inches of stem. Tie a bow with the ribbon and secure the flower in the knot. I used kalanchoe, a very colorful and hearty succulent, but I'm also partial to lavender. Tie the ribbons and flowers all around the picnic basket, spacing them evenly apart.

Floral-Wrapped Sandwiches

I told you I don't cook. I don't even make sandwiches. These sandwiches are from my supermarket deli, but when wrapped in beautiful floral fabrics and topped off with sprigs of lilac, they look absolutely heavenly. I think Miss Austen would approve.

Party Tip

If you're having an outdoor party, raid your closet and have some extra sweatshirts and sweaters handy in case your guests get cold. They'll appreciate the warm gesture.

❋ PART 2 ❋

HOLIDAY SPECIALS

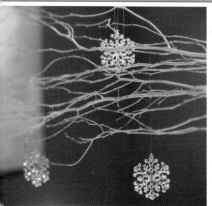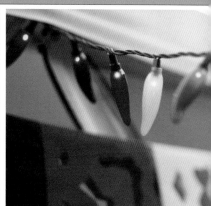

I'm not sure how a lot of holidays originated or how they came to be conveniently spaced throughout the year, but I'm sure glad they exist. While holidays tend to be celebrated in traditional ways, the following chapters present some novel touches to mark the festivities. Keep in mind that you can always match the parties in this book with different holidays. For example, I've thrown the Pink Party, presented in Chapter 10 for Breast Cancer Awareness Month, for New Year's Eve; the Spoon-Bending Party in Chapter 11 doesn't have to occur during Halloween; and the Paris Flea Market Party from Chapter 1 would be perfect for a variety of occasions, like Valentine's Day or Mother's Day. It's your party, and you can mix and match if you want to.

CHAPTER 6

Winter Wonderland

A White Christmas to Remember

I'm a holiday fanatic. I have four aluminum Christmas trees, two of which are silver, one blue, and one pink. I know every Christmas carol by heart, I know how to replace defective bulbs on strands of lights, and, although I don't own a Santa suit, my dog, Broadway, has two of them. I particularly enjoy this time of year, because it gives me a chance to catch up with friends. It's amazing how everyone's kids keep getting older every year, while I stay so young!

When I was a kid, one of my favorite things to do at Christmastime was to look at all the holiday window displays at the mall. The tableaus of snow, elves, and animals seemed to be so real, like I could jump right in and live in their fantasy world. (I just knew that when the mall was closed, all those creatures in the window came to life.) This winter party is a celebration and homage to those scenic play lands, updated, of course, with an elegant white-on-white theme.

Snow Globe Invitation

What a sparkling way to invite friends to your party! Everyone loves snow globes, and these customized ones will put your guests in the holiday spirit. You can purchase do-it-yourself snow globes at crafts stores and stationery stores. The bottom cover snaps off, and you just slide your invitation inside. The water magnifies the words, as snow flurries hint at the wonders to come.

Snow Tableau

Yes, you too can have a snow-covered winter fantasy running the length of your dining room table. Even your most jaded party guests will raise an eyebrow of admiration over this display. All it takes is some instant snow powder and some acrylic photo frames.

1 Instant snow is fun and easy to make. I bought the snow powder at the mall during the holidays, but I've listed the manufacturer's website in the Resource Directory on page 158. Place a small scoop of snow powder into a cup, add water, and the snow forms instantly. It's cool to the touch. It lasts for a couple of weeks and will revert to its powder form, at which time it's even reusable. As you make each scoop, place the snow in a large bowl. One box of the powder makes almost two gallons of snow.

2 Line the center of your table with 11- x 14-inch acrylic photo frames facing upside down so that the frames can hold snow. A typical sixty-inch dining table will hold four frames lengthwise.

3 Pour snow into the frames, distributing it evenly between them. Next, place various decorative elements in the snow, like reindeer, penguins, gifts, or even tableware such as martini shakers. Then sprinkle more snow on top of the decorations.

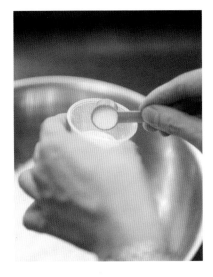

Winter Branches

Adding to the whimsy of this winter wonderland, white branches float above the dining room table, as if a magic tree had lent you its branches for the evening. It's a dramatic visual statement and also the first thing people will notice when they see your table.

If I had to name a signature element of my parties, I'd have to say it's the "floating centerpiece." In fact, many of the parties in this book feature floating centerpieces such as this one. When I was creating the parties for this book, my photographer, Jessica, would say, "Okay, what are we hanging today?" The space above your dining room table is valuable real estate, but no one ever uses it. I love to hang things from the ceiling, because it doesn't take up space on the table or obstruct sight lines. And, it's so unexpected, guests immediately say, "Wow!"

WHAT YOU'LL NEED
3 or 4 white branches
Hot glue gun
Fishing line
3M Cord Clips with
Command Adhesive
Silver ornaments

1 The branches pictured are birch branches (actually twigs that have been painted white). You can purchase similar branches at any craft store. If they're not already painted, just use spray paint to get the same effect. You can also start with branches you might have in your yard.

2 Using a hot glue gun, attach three or four branches to each other. This step gives you a fuller decoration, and the hot glue keeps the branches from flying all over the place.

3 Tie fishing line to two ends of the branches and hang from the ceiling. I recommend 3M Cord Clips with Command Adhesive as ceiling hooks, because they can be removed easily without damaging your paint. As you can see in the photo, I have a whole network of these 3M Cord Clips above my own dining table at all times, so I'm always ready to hang decorations.

4 Hang a few silver ornaments from the branches to complete the "Wow!" factor.

Snow Hurricanes

I often have a problem with wax from my candles dripping onto the table. Placing the candlesticks in cylindrical glass vases eliminates this problem, and the look is very clean and modern. Pour some instant snow into the vases, and you have a wintry version of hurricane lamps.

Snowflake Sandwiches

As an appetizer before the main course, these wintry finger sandwiches delight the eyes and palate. With a snowflake or star cookie cutter, trim your bread into holiday shapes. Then fill with your favorite spreads, vegetables, or meats. Serve the sandwiches on plates lined with coconut shavings, which resemble snow.

Fur-Wrapped Candles

It's the holidays, so you really must send your guests off with a lovely parting gift. This luxurious party favor of white candles wrapped in faux fur will look brilliant on your white-on-white holiday table as well.

1 Cut the faux fur into eight-inch squares, removing all the fuzz from the edges. There's no need to sew the fur.

2 Wrap the fur around two white candles, and tie a white or silver ribbon around the whole thing. Place one set of candles on each place setting, so your guests know they should've brought you a host gift.

Party Tip

Be sure to mark containers for trash and recyclables. You don't want your guests looking all over your house for a garbage can. For holiday parties, I like to find large, empty cardboard boxes and wrap them in festive paper. Then I place oversized gift tags on the boxes, labeling them "trash," "glass," and "plastic."

CHAPTER 7

It's Easy Being Green

A St. Patrick's Party That's Good for the Environment

I know. St. Patrick's Day is supposed to be about green beer, leprechauns, green beer, the luck of the Irish, green beer, getting pinched if you don't wear green, and green beer. For a change, give your St. Patty's party a twist by giving new meaning to green. As in eco-friendly, "let's be kind to the earth" green. There's no better time to remind friends and family that the world we live in is a precious one, and one that needs to be respected and cared for. Don't worry; I'm not going to get all Birkenstock on you, but I do think that if we think green, the luck of the Irish may stay with us just a little bit longer.

I encourage you to celebrate the day with all the gusto you normally would, but incorporate some of the ideas from the following pages. Use this opportunity to educate people on easy ways they can make a difference. By introducing these ideas in the context of a party, you're sending a message that being environmentally aware doesn't have to be difficult or boring. Okay, I'm stepping off my recycled soapbox now and putting on my green pants.

Planting the Seeds

Plant the seeds to your party by slipping an invitation in a seed packet. Just cut open the top of the packet and place your invitation inside. If the seeds are large enough, you can leave them in the packet. If they're small, they will easily fall out of the envelope, so take them out first and save them for your guests in a separate envelope.

Recycling Central

Since I have so many used ink cartridges lying around my home office, this party is the perfect excuse to get them all together for recycling. Tell friends to bring their used ink cartridges, batteries, and magazines and set up a mini recycling center at your party. Label some baskets with the appropriate recyclable and let the filling begin. Look in the yellow pages or online for your local recycling facility. I've also listed a helpful website in the Resource Directory on page 158.

Place Card Tips

Instead of place cards that have friends' names on them, write environmental tips on the cards, and have each person share them at the table. Here are some ideas for tips you can include:

- Use reusable coffee filters rather than paper ones. Imagine all the coffee filters being tossed away every day.
- Replace paper towels with a cloth towel you can wash and reuse.
- Buy products in bulk to save on packaging.
- When ordering take-out food, don't take the plastic utensils that they offer you.
- Order ice cream in a cone instead of a cup. It's so much more fun, anyway.
- When you're shopping at the mall, put all your purchases in one bag rather than getting a new one at each store.
- Donate your used clothing and household goods to charity instead of throwing them away.
- Donate unused paint to schools and local theater companies.
- Save papers that you've printed on once and print on the other side.
- Purchase rechargeable batteries.
- Eat less meat. The cultivation of livestock is one of the largest sources of greenhouse gases.
- Set a goal to reduce energy consumption by 20 percent from last year.
- Conserve water by switching to low-flow toilets and showerheads.
- At work, have everyone bring unwanted dishes and silverware to replace the disposable plates and utensils in the break room.

Bamboo Plates

Bamboo is not a tree. It's a grass. Unlike trees, when bamboo stalks are cut, more sprout out in their place. That's why bamboo is environmentally friendly. I found these bamboo plates and thought they'd be perfect for a green party. They're lightweight yet still surprisingly sturdy. Look for other bamboo products you can use in your own home.

Plant a Tree

As your guests leave, give each one a tree that they can take home and plant. Trees create fresh air and absorb pollutants. You can also plant a tree in your yard together and year after year track the growth of the tree you've "adopted." And, of course, toast its growth with a glass of green beer.

Leprechaun Snacks

These hors d'oeuvres of raw, organic vegetables wrapped in greens are so beautiful—and tasty—that they might just convert confirmed carnivores. Julienned slivers of carrots and cucumbers are nestled with pumpkin sprouts in colorful red kale and then tied up with a chive.

The secret to tying the chive is to dip it in hot water first to relax it; otherwise, the chive will break. For an impressive presentation, lay these snacks on a flat of fresh wheat grass.

Party Tip

For any party, try to serve foods that taste good cold or at room temperature. It will save you the trouble of heating food all night. You can also prepare food the day before and not have to worry about reheating.

CHAPTER 8

¡Viva the Party!

An Outdoor Cinco de Mayo Celebration

I used to think that Cinco de Mayo was Mexican Independence Day. It's a common misconception. The holiday actually commemorates the victory of the Mexican army over the French at the Battle of the Puebla in 1862. Sprinkle that tidbit of knowledge into a conversation at your next cocktail party and you're sure to make a favorable impression, unless, of course, you're talking to someone who's French.

Growing up in California, we had Cinco de Mayo parties as early as kindergarten. I remember how my teacher brought in a piñata, telling us we had to hit it with a stick to let all the candies out. Ever the efficiency expert, I wondered why she just didn't give us the candy outright so that we didn't ruin a perfectly good piñata, but I soon discovered the destructive activity was a lot of fun. In my Cinco de Mayo party, I also use piñatas, but in a much more decorative way. I have a feeling even the French would approve.

Piñata Invitation

This mini piñata from a party supply store is a *muy* colorful way to announce your fiesta. Using a sharp knife, cut a slit in the top of the piñata and slip your invitation inside.

Adobe Taco Station

I'm always looking for new ways to present everyday food. Shown is a strawberry pot from the nursery, which is usually used to plant herbs and such. I thought the little compartments would be perfect for taco fixings.

1 Line each compartment of the strawberry pot with aluminum foil, keeping the foil secure with duct tape on the inside. You will have little aluminum bowls when you're finished.

2 Fill each compartment with lettuce, cheese, salsa, guacamole, and other taco accoutrements.

3 The top of the strawberry pot is the perfect size for a bowl of meat.

Party Tip

Place a small container of individually wrapped toothpicks on the buffet table, at the bar, and even the bathroom, along with a small hand mirror, so that your guests can check their teeth. I'm always horrified when I've returned home from a party only to realize that I've had an entire farm stuck between my two front teeth all night.

Piñata Florals

Here's a way to celebrate with piñatas without whacking them. As you can see, they make delightful vessels for fresh flowers. You can even save them and reuse them in the future.

1 Punch a hole in various spots of the piñata with a steak knife.

2 Insert flower stems into water tubes, available at floral supply stores. Push the water tubes into the holes. (If you use heartier flowers, such as sunflowers, you don't need to put them into the water tubes. Just put the stem directly into the piñata.) .

Patron Candles

I really love those tall glass patron candles that you find at supermarkets in the Mexican food aisle. They come in vibrant colors, and they're super cheap. Imagine how your party guests will flip when they find patron candles personalized with their photos, proclaiming them to be guardians of whatever hobby or quirk they may be known for.

1   Look for glass patron candles without any artwork on them. If you can only find ones with labels, just peel the labels off.

2   Using a computer graphic software program such as Photoshop, create a 4- x 6-inch image of your friends' faces, along with their appropriate saint designation.

3   Adhere the image to a patron candle with a glue stick. I made a patron candle of "Our Lady of the Perpetual Skates" for my friend Drake in New York, and I could hear her laughter all the way here in California.

It's Chili Out Here

I'm sure you may have a box of Christmas lights that come out only once a year. I decided one year to start displaying them year-round by popping multicolored chili pepper covers onto the bulbs. I bought a whole bag of the covers online, and now I'm tempted to cover everyone's lights with these spicy decorations.

Fiesta Banners

My version of the traditional Mexican flag banner incorporates fabric instead of tissue paper. The fabric adds weight to the banner, helping it stay in place if a sudden wind gust should kick up. You can also keep the flags and reuse them for a future party.

1 Cut fabrics of different colors into pieces that are approximately 7 x 18 inches. (I used inexpensive cotton twills.) You'll want 8 to 10 fabric pieces per banner, depending on how long it is.

2 Fold a piece in half to create a flag that's about 7 x 9 inches. Now pretend you're making a snowflake. Fold the fabric over and over again and cut designs into the folded fabric. Try folding the fabrics differently to create various patterns. For some, fold straight up and down; for others, fold diagonally.

3 Unfold the flags to their 7 x 9 size to reveal your fun cutout patterns.

4 Tie a string or cord across trees or posts. Drape the flags on the string.

CHAPTER 9

Starfish and Stripes

Fourth of July by the Sea

For me, the ultimate way to spend the Fourth of July is to celebrate at my summer rental in the Hamptons. There's nothing like sipping lemonade by the pool or mingling with my famous neighbors, as we watch fireworks from my private beach. Not that I have a place in the Hamptons, or have even stepped foot on the shores, but I've watched all those *Sex and the City* episodes, so I feel like I'm practically a local. Still, it's easy to create a seaside Independence Day party, even if you're nowhere near the sea.

I was originally going to set this celebration outside, but reconsidered when I remembered so many of my friends live in condos or apartments, where they don't even have a patio. So I decided to bring the beach inside. It's proof that you don't have to own a private beach to feel patriotic—but if I did, I sure would be one happy American.

Cool Shades

Let your guests know it's going to be a sunny affair by putting the party details on a pair of sunglasses. You can find cheap sunglasses at a party store. They're sold as props, without the UV coating, so you won't feel like you're wasting a perfectly good pair of sunglasses. Print the invitation on paper, and then adhere it to the lenses with a glue stick.

Starfish-Spangled Banner

Guess what, the red and white tablecloth pictured is actually a striped rug from Ikea. I've seen a lot of rugs that I thought would make good tablecloths through my travels. They add texture to the table, and they're usually easy to spot clean. I completed the star-spangled look by adding a strip of blue denim, topped with some starfish.

Seashell Arrangements

Place one of these floral seashells on each plate for a vibrant place setting.

1. Buy small seashells that have a cavity.

2. Carve a small piece of floral foam that will fit in the cavity.

3. Dip the foam in water until it's completely wet, and place it in the seashell.

4. Insert flowers into the foam. I chose an all-red theme, to play off the blue plates and white napkins.

Shell Bowls

Shells make ideal serving bowls for condiments. Even old standbys like ketchup and mustard become classier. This is an idea you'll certainly relish—okay, I couldn't resist. I bought these shells at a restaurant supply store. If you purchase regular shells that weren't intended for food, be sure to wash them thoroughly to make them food-safe.

Fishing for Compliments

This fishing net festooned with flowers adds a cool nautical touch to a party. You can find fishing nets at craft- and party-supply stores. They come in their natural color, as well as bright Day-Glo colors.

1 Hang a fishing net above your table with the help of our good friend, the 3M Cord Clips.

2 In the patriotic spirit, your catch of the day won't be any kind of fish but rather red, white, and blue silk flowers. Stems of silk flowers are usually made of stiff wire, so you'll need wire cutters or metal snips to cut the stem. Just leave about two inches on the stems and hook them into the net, as shown above.

Sand Candles

In this table decoration, layers of red, white, and blue sand nestle a candle in a holder. These long-stemmed candleholders add height and drama to a table, but you can use any glass container you like.

1 Slowly pour one color of sand at a time into the candleholder.

2 Place the candle on top of the sand, gently pushing down on it to keep it in place.

Red, White, and Cool

These ice cubes are just too fun. The red ones are made with cranberry juice, the white with regular water, and the blue with Gatorade. I have a vague memory from high school science class that different liquids have different freezing points, so expect the colored ice cubes to take a bit longer to freeze.

Think Pink

A Pink Party for Breast Cancer Awareness Month

You may have heard the statistic that every three minutes a woman in the United States is diagnosed with breast cancer, or that the chances of a woman developing breast cancer during her lifetime are approximately one in eight. But those are just numbers. On a human level, the toll of breast cancer is much more devastating. I don't know anyone who has not been personally affected by this disease. My sister was diagnosed with it, as was my sister-in-law and so many of my friends and their sisters and mothers.

On the positive side, increased awareness of breast cancer has led to earlier detection and treatment, which has saved lives. October is Breast Cancer Awareness Month, and the color pink has become the galvanizing hue to raise awareness, promote early detection, and search for a cure. In fact, pink-colored products like blenders and cupcake molds are available year-round to keep breast cancer at the forefront of people's minds. Pink is one of my favorite colors, and I'm secure enough in my masculinity to wear it. So in the spirit of thinking pink, this chapter presents a party that not only promotes breast cancer awareness but also celebrates the courage of the women touched by it.

This invitation, also designed for me by the Card Club Ladies, uses the iris-folding technique of overlapping folded papers in a circular pattern so that the inside looks like the iris of a camera or eye. I think the pink papers in the heart perfectly capture the feeling of the party. Iris folding looks very complicated, but when you see the reverse side of the invitation, it's evident how simple it is to pull off.

1 Cut the pink card stock to the desired size of your invitation. The one pictured opposite is 5½ x 4¼ inches. If you'd like, cut diagonals at the top to vary the shape.

2 Cut the white card stock to a size that's smaller than the pink card stock. You will be doing the iris folding on the white card.

3 Cut a heart shape into the white card stock. On the front side, stamp the background with a floral stamp.

4 Fold the one-inch strips of wrapping paper in half lengthwise and tape each strip on the back side of the white card stock. Tape the strips down in a twirling pattern as shown at left. You can alter the pattern however you'd like by taping the strips down in various configurations. However, all folds should face the inside of the heart. Turn the heart over periodically to check your design. The back will look very messy, but don't worry; no one will see the back. If your paper strips have gone past the edge of the card stock, just trim them with scissors. Now turn the white card face up and glue it onto the pink card.

5 Stamp "Celebrate Life" onto the pink card stock, or just write it in. On the opposite side of the invitation, you can print out the party details.

6 Punch a hole at the top and thread pink and white ribbon through it.

Places, Everyone

I wanted to spruce up the walls in the dining area, yet still keep with the pink theme, so I decided to install a temporary wall treatment made of plastic place mats. The place mats are strung together with ball chain key chains and then hooked to the wall with 3M Cord Clips (regular 3M Command Strip Hooks also work fine).

1 Drill a small hole on opposite ends of each place mat, about a half inch from the edge.

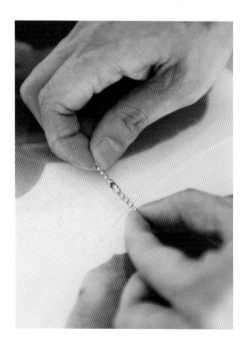

2 String place mats to each other with ball chain key chains, threading the chain through the holes you've drilled. Attach three to four place mats per row.

3 On one end of your place mat strand, thread a chain through the hole and hook the entire row onto the 3M Cord Clip.

Falling Petals

These silk rose petals suspended on thread create quite an effect over a dining room table. When you move quickly around the table, keeping your eyes on the petals, it looks like the scene from *The Matrix* in which the characters are floating in the air in suspended animation. You can purchase rose petals at your local craft store, usually in the wedding supplies aisle.

1   String petals on a piece of pink thread, spacing them about eight inches apart. Make some strands shorter, with about three petals, and others longer, with up to six petals. Apply a dab of white glue where the thread meets the petals, to keep them from sliding down.

2   Placing small dabs of poster putty at the top end of the thread, adhere the strands of rose petals to the ceiling.

An Absolute Frill

Pink feather boas wrapped around chargers add a soft, playful texture to table settings. The feather boas available at craft stores are typically six feet long. Cut them in half, and circle the boas around the edge of the chargers.

Pink and Brownie

This cupcake sundae looks fancy and hard to make, but it requires absolutely no baking or mixing. Just eating and smiling.

1 Start with a pre-made chocolate muffin. Cut the muffin top off and save it for later.

2 Cut about a half inch off the top of the remaining base of the muffin. Eat that piece, since you won't need it anymore.

3 Using a cookie cutter that's the same diameter as your muffin base, scoop up about a half inch of strawberry ice cream. Layer this scoop on top of the muffin base. The ice cream takes the place of the muffin piece that you just ate, and no one will be the wiser.

4 Position the muffin top on the ice cream layer. Spread store-bought white icing on the muffin top.

5 Roll out a piece of pre-made pink fondant (one pack comes with four colors) and slice a piece that's about ¼ inch x 5 inches long. Make a pink ribbon out of the fondant and place it on top of the white icing.

Orchids in Jelly Beans

Pink jellybeans in champagne glasses make pinkalicious party favors, especially when they're topped with an orchid.

1 Fill the champagne glass halfway with jellybeans, and then place an orchid in a water tube and into the glass. Note that the water tube isn't really to keep the orchid fresh but to keep the stem away from the jellybeans. These favors look so beautiful on the table that you may be reluctant to part with them, but please give them away—it's easy to make more.

Party Tip

Ask guests to bring a small donation made out to Susan G. Komen for the Cure or the American Cancer Society. Have them place their checks in an envelope that's already addressed to the charities, so that their donations can remain private.

CHAPTER II

Spellbound

A Halloween Spoon-Bending Party

I have a beef about Halloween. Frankly, the whole idea of monsters, witches, and slasher gore doesn't make sense to me as party material. What's so fun about death, psychosis, and demons? Be honest, if an actual zombie wielding a machete were to appear at your doorstep, would you really be in such a party mood? Nope, didn't think so. That kind of visit would certainly kill the party—in more ways than one.

The mysterious and unexplainable are much more interesting to me as Halloween fodder. Think levitation, mind over matter, and *The Twilight Zone*. They're still strange and fantastical, but, importantly, they don't threaten to behead me. So expand your mind and enter the realm of the metaphysical. And leave the scares and screams for another holiday—like Boss's Day.

Disappearing Act

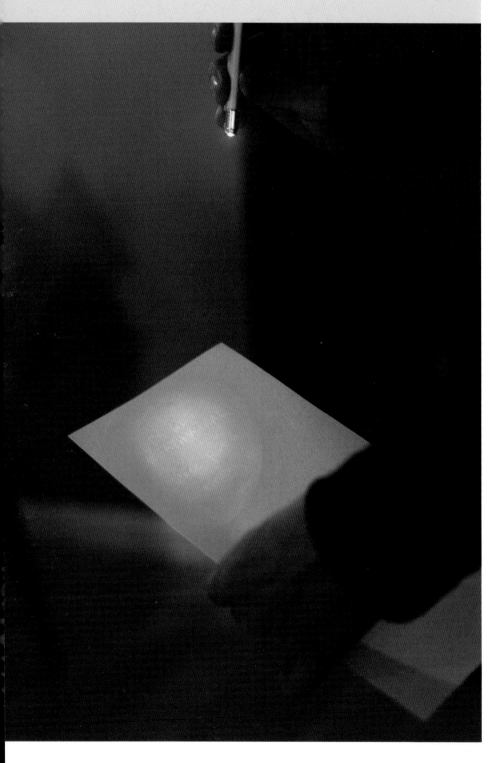

Invisible ink is one of the world's greatest inventions. I'd put it up there with the cotton gin and the Ab Roller. It's so much fun, and I don't understand why people only use it for practical purposes, like writing security information on electronic equipment. Snooze. I wish I could write checks with it—that would teach the cable company.

Here's the most perfect way to use invisible ink: on your party invitation. When you send your friends a sheet of paper with nothing written on it, they might think you're a little nutty, but they'll think you're crazy with creativity when they realize that your message is invisible. It's so Houdini. Be sure to include a pen with a UV lamp so that they can read the invitation. Most invisible ink pens have a built-in UV lamp, so they serve both functions.

Mysterious Hands

These gloved hands, acting on their own without bodies, are inspired by the Jean Cocteau version of *Beauty and the Beast*. Cocteau's classic film has a scene that depicts candelabras held by disembodied hands, and the haunting image has always stayed with me. Of course, these hands also remind me of Thing from *The Addams Family*. Also, with the magic of pipe cleaners, you can make these hands hold place cards.

1   Purchase black mittens. Stuff the inside of the mittens with tissue paper, along with a pipe cleaner in each of the fingers and the thumb.

2   Bend the index finger until it touches the thumb and place a card between them.

The main event of this party is spoon bending. When people hear about that phenomenon, they immediately become skeptical. They think it's either a hoax or, worse, tied to some cult. But spoon bending is actually a scientific matter. Your mind creates energy. Just because you don't see the energy doesn't mean it doesn't exist. You don't see microwaves or wireless internet signals, but you know they're working.

Jack Houck, an aeronautics and aerospace engineer, has personally introduced this phenomenon to over 18,000 people in what he calls "PK Parties." PK stands for psychokinesis, or mind over matter. In these parties, he guides the group into performing a "kindergarten" level of psychokinesis, which involves holding a metal object, such as a spoon or fork, making it turn soft in your hands, and then twisting the metal around and around like a pretzel. Mr. Houck estimates that about 85 percent of the participants at these parties are able to bend the metal.

I've been to one of Mr. Houck's events, and I bent spoons—lots of them, along with a few forks. The spoons and forks in the photo are actual utensils that I bent. Skeptics would say that I did it with sheer strength, but they obviously have not seen my skinny wrists. Regardless of how strong you may be, you cannot make a spoon melt and twist in curly-cues or make fork tines splay out like a fan, which is what I did. If I were strong enough to bend a spoon, then I would be able to bend the metal back to its original shape, but I couldn't after the metal hardened again.

Besides the entertaining aspect of spoon bending, this party is really about experiencing what we believe to be impossible and about reducing the limitations we place upon ourselves. We can accomplish a lot, as long as we set our minds to it.

So how do you perform psycho kinesis? Mr. Houck outlines a very specific process. Gather at least fifteen people together. Have everyone sit in a circle, with a facilitator standing in the middle to lead the group. It's great to have children over five years old at these parties, because they have not put as many limitations upon themselves as we have. The facilitator walks the group through the following three steps:

1. **Connect Your Mind to What You Want** With everyone holding a spoon in their hands, Mr. Houck instructs his guests to "Get a point of concentration in your head. Focus it to a point. Then grab it; bring it down through your head, neck, shoulder, arm, and hand; and put it into place where you want the silverware to bend."

2. **Command the Metal to Bend** On the count of three, everyone shouts the word "BEND" three times. This step feels silly to a lot of people. Silly is good, as I'll explain later. Mr. Houck claims that for a paranormal experience to happen, you must deliberately create a "peak emotional event," because the mind locks onto peak emotional encounters. If everyone shouts at the top of their lungs to create as much noise and excitement as possible, it will hopefully be the biggest emotional event that has ever happened at that place at any time. This will cause everyone's minds to lock onto the phenomenon at that very moment. In layman's terms, you're getting the energy going.

3. **Release the Thought** Now just let it happen. Remember that at this kindergarten level of pychokinesis the spoon isn't twisting on its own. You're bending it manually–but not with force. The metal will turn soft and rubbery, and your hands are just there to help bend it. Some people keep furrowing their brows and concentrating, wondering why their spoons aren't bending. They need to divert their attention elsewhere. That's why people acting silly in Step 2 is so important. All the giggling and noise become distractions—distractions that allow you to release the thought. As more and more people around the room start bending their spoons, the shouting and the jumping help distract everyone else.

I've listed Mr. Houck's website in the Resource Directory on page 158 so that you can read up more on it. Just remember to have fun and that it's fun to be silly! And, if you're not able to bend spoons on your first try, don't worry. At my first PK party, I was the only one who was unsuccessful at the task. But at my next party, I was bending spoons like a superhero!

Upright Fork Skewers

We've already got hands standing by themselves, napkins floating, and spoons twisting like rubber. Now let's serve appetizers on forks that rise out of a bowl. Again, these appetizers are from the frozen food aisle.

1 Place dry floral foam in a serving bowl.

2 Insert forks in the foam, lining them up in a straight line.

3 Skewer your appetizers onto the fork tines. Cover the foam with a piece of black fabric.

Party Tip

I usually have so much extra food that I'm begging people to take it home. Purchase some recyclable plastic or foil food containers for guests to take home leftovers. With plenty of containers handy, they'll know you're serious.

Floating Centerpiece

A row of stark white calla lilies floating above the table may look surreal, but they also form a practical centerpiece, since they don't take up space on the table. Although silk calla lilies are in the photo, I've also used real ones, which will stay fresh looking for about thirty-six hours out of water. Tie some fishing line around the base of the flowers and hang them from 3M Cord Clips on the ceiling.

Flying Napkins

This party really defies gravity. I'm sure this is the first time any of your guests will have seen napkins floating above their place setting—it sure beats napkin rings.

1. Hang the napkins, just as I did the calla lilies above, except use thread instead of fishing line, as thread works better with cloth napkins.

2. Before dinner is served, snip the threads to release the napkins, or, better yet, leave them floating so your guests can just lean in and wipe their mouths.

❋ PART 3 ❋

EXCLUSIVE ENGAGEMENTS

Not too many people know it, but I used to be a comedy cabaret performer. I had quite a few fans of my show "You Can't Go Wrong with Johnny Fong." There's nothing like working a live audience. When you have them in the palm of your hand, you can do or say anything, and they're rolling in the aisles. My love of performing is probably why I love to throw parties. I'm always looking for new ways to put smiles on people's faces. In this last group of parties, I've showcased themes that are not related to any holiday or occasion. Instead, they're parties for the sake of parties. The entertainment value is amped up, and each one is a showstopper.

CHAPTER 12

Breakfast at Jonathan's

Diamonds Are a Bagel's Best Friend

When I first saw the movie *Breakfast at Tiffany's*, I totally related to Audrey Hepburn's character of Holly Golightly. She came from humble origins; I came from Hong Kong. Her life was one big party; I liked to plan parties. And like her, I've also eaten in front of Tiffany & Co., although I had a hot dog instead of a Danish.

To Holly, Tiffany's was the epitome of happiness. While I'm just as happy at Target, I do understand the allure of the famous jewelry store. The mere sight of a blue box with white ribbon is enough to make otherwise rational human beings shriek with joy. That's why this party is so much fun. It evokes a sense of luxury and sophistication that would make Holly Golightly feel quite at home. Yet, with giant diamond rings humorously dangling above the table, this is hardly a stuffy affair.

This chapter is also a reminder that not all parties need to be scheduled for afternoons or evenings. Breakfast gatherings are great, because they start the day off in such a festive fashion, and your guests still have the remainder of the day to run errands or relax—or maybe buy you a nice thank-you gift at Tiffany's.

Silver-Plated Invitation

What an elegant way to announce your breakfast party! Just slip your invitation in a silver frame. I buy frames en masse at discount stores. Print out your invitation on white paper and glue it onto a larger piece of blue paper so that you have about a half-inch border.

Jewelry Box Orchids

There's something quite thrilling about black velvet jewelry boxes. They hold the promise of valuable gems and eternal love. The moment the box is opened is as exciting as when the briefcases in the TV show *Deal or No Deal* are opened. Everyone's heart just skips a beat.

These boxes are also lovely on place settings, holding cymbidium orchids as shown. As I've mentioned before, orchids are hearty flowers. The cymbidium orchids from this photo shoot lasted for days out of water; and when they began to droop, I dropped them into a bowl of water and they were resuscitated instantly. See, true love conquers all.

Blue-and-White Centerpieces

White flowers in distinctive blue-and-white gift boxes are gorgeous centerpieces that pay tribute to the real thing. While they make quite an impact at this breakfast party, I can imagine these arrangements gracing the tables of wedding receptions and bridal showers as well.

1 Find an empty box without a lid and wrap it with light blue paper.

2 Tape white ribbon to each side of the package.

3 Place a container filled with wet floral foam in the box. You can also use a container with water, but you must be careful not to spill it, or the package will become wet.

4 Insert stems of white flowers in the box. If you are displaying several packages, use a different type of white flower in each box, as shown in the photo above.

Giant Diamond Rings

Your party will be dripping in diamonds with these oversized diamond rings hanging above your table. In my book *Flowers that Wow*, I created a simple floral arrangement similar to these rings, using a white rose as the diamond. Here, the diamonds are made of water faucet handles. You will never look at a bathroom sink the same way again.

WHAT YOU'LL NEED FOR ONE RING
7- or 10-inch embroidery hoop (pictured are a combination of both sizes)
Drill
Wood glue
Spray primer paint
Spray silver metallic paint
Clear faucet handle
Size #8-32 x 2-inch screw and nut
Screwdriver
Fishing line
3 M Cord Clip

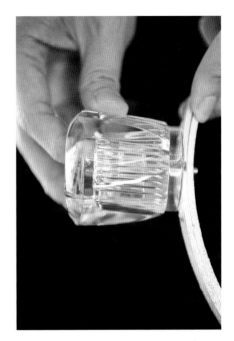

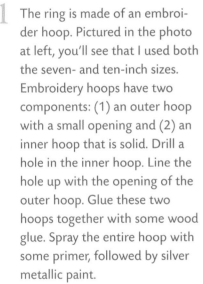

1 The ring is made of an embroider hoop. Pictured in the photo at left, you'll see that I used both the seven- and ten-inch sizes. Embroidery hoops have two components: (1) an outer hoop with a small opening and (2) an inner hoop that is solid. Drill a hole in the inner hoop. Line the hole up with the opening of the outer hoop. Glue these two hoops together with some wood glue. Spray the entire hoop with some primer, followed by silver metallic paint.

2 To attach the faucet handle to the hoop, use a size #8-32 x 2-inch screw with a corresponding nut. Flip off the "hot" or "cold" lid of the faucet handle, slide the screw inside, and let it pass through the hole in the embroidery hoop.

3 Fasten the screw with the nut and replace the lid of the faucet. Tie fishing line to the ring and hang it from the ceiling using 3M Cord Clips.

Velvet Place Mats

Jewelers use black velvet jewelry pads to display diamonds because they make the gems stand out. I've followed the same principle and created these velvet place mats that will set off your china beautifully. I also scattered some acrylic gems around the place settings to add even more sparkle.

1 Take a fifteen-inch square of foam core and wrap it in velvet. Secure the velvet on the back side with duct tape.

Tea Service

A mirrored jewelry box becomes a classy, yet practical serving tray for an array of teas. The tea bags can be displayed in the various drawers, and the bags can be hung from the jewelry hooks.

Party Tip

Host an after-party after your main party later that evening, or even the next day. Take advantage of the fact that you already have all the decorations up, the centerpieces are still fresh, there's extra food and drinks in the fridge, and the house has never been so clean. You've gone through all the trouble already, so have some other friends over to enjoy your efforts!

CHAPTER 13

Come to the Cabaret

Where the Guests Do the Entertaining

I will sing at the drop of a hat. A few years ago, I was at the movies, and the theater manager made an announcement that anyone who sang a Broadway show tune in front of the whole audience would receive a free movie poster. I didn't even hear the part about the free movie poster. My hand went up immediately, because I welcome any chance to sing in front of a captive audience. (In case you were wondering, I sang "As If We Never Said Goodbye" from *Sunset Boulevard*.) I'm not alone in my zeal to perform. People love to be on stage. Witness the popularity of karaoke bars. In this era of *American Idol*, everyone wants to be a rock star.

In fact, the best party I've ever thrown was a talent show party. I turned my living room into a cabaret and invited friends to perform. Several of them sang, one played the cello, one did stand-up comedy, and another juggled and balanced a wheelbarrow on his chin. I had no idea that my friends had such hidden talents. But the real reason the party was such a success was that it was participatory. The evening was about more than drinking and eating. Even if they weren't sharing their talents on stage, those in the audience were active players, just in the simple act of enjoying the performances and applauding. Talent, it seemed, was the ultimate icebreaker.

VIP Ticket

Invite your guests to the cabaret party by sending them VIP tickets. Granted, everyone will be a VIP, but you don't have to tell them that! Create your ticket with a desktop publishing program and print copies on glossy paper. Be sure to make the tickets oversized so that they make a bigger impact.

TIPS ON PRODUCING A CABARET NIGHT

- Ask friends at least a full month before the party whether they would like to participate, so that they have plenty of time to practice.
- You must perform. It will set an example for other guests.
- All performers should be "booked" in advance. Don't expect, or even allow, spur-of-the-moment performers.
- Do not have any sort of judging or awards. It's a celebration, not a competition.
- Have it videotaped so you have a record of the evening.
- Hire a pianist for the night to accompany singers, as well as to play background music before and after the show. Give performers the option of rehearsing with the pianist, at their expense.
- Establish a performance line-up order and stay on schedule. Try to vary the talent, so you don't lump all the singers together at one time.
- Either be the emcee yourself or have a friend fill the role. Give him or her the line-up.
- Give a rose to each performer at the end of each performance.

Making an Entrance

Rather than having performers step out of the audience, have them in a backstage area, which in my case is the kitchen. Cordon off the area with a red velvet curtain, so each performer can make a big entrance when his or her name is called. As you can see, I used a tension rod for a shower curtain and hung a red velvet drapery panel on it.

Footlights

Define the stage area, usually the front of a living room, with rope lighting. A fifteen-foot strand is enough to create a big enough stage, unless there's a major dance number happening. Rope lighting right out of the box is tightly wound up, so stretch it out overnight to relax it a bit. Then adhere it to the floor in a rectangular shape, using wide, clear packaging tape.

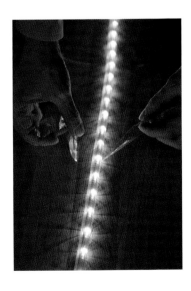

Table For Two

I shudder when I see wood "decorator round tables" used as night stands.
They are the worst idea in decorating. However, I do recommend them for
cocktail tables at your cabaret night. Just two situated in the front are enough
to create a nightclub feel. Drape the tables with a black tablecloth and you
have instant atmosphere.

Personalized Napkins

Your own cabaret deserves its own napkins. Go to your local office supply store and have them make you a custom stamp for less than $20. Name your joint, pick a typeface, and stamp the logo onto the cocktail napkins. Be sure to use a stamp pad that has nontoxic ink.

Presenting the Platters

Vinyl records make artful platters for the evening's appetizers. You'll want to wash them first, of course. Because records are so thin, they are hard to handle when they sit directly on a table, so raise them by displaying them on a cake stand or even a bowl turned upside down. Also, keep them away from candlelight, as the candles will melt the vinyl.

Party Tip

If you're displaying a variety of hors d'oeuvres, place a folded card next to each and write down its name. People like to know what they're eating.

CHAPTER 14

Vroom to Party

A Grand Prix Festival

I'll admit, I'm not the biggest car buff. I once took an auto mechanics class, and the only thing I learned was that it's worth it to pay someone else to change the oil in your car. But auto racing, that's another matter. I grew up on Hot Wheels. I had miles of the plastic orange track and a whole collection of miniature cars, which I stored in my tire-shaped car caddie. Of course, my most prized Hot Wheels were the Sizzlers that I would juice up with power so they'd race on their own. They were like magic. Now I like to take my Mini Cooper for a spin and hug the curves of the winding Sepulveda pass in Los Angeles. Going 45 miles per hour, I may not be a Formula One champion; but in my mind, I'm the cartoon character Speed Racer, with my pet chimpanzee Chim-Chim in the passenger seat—actually my dog, Broadway.

The race-inspired party in this chapter is perfect for your next NASCAR-watching gathering, but it's also fun for almost any occasion. After all, who hasn't gripped their hands around a steering wheel and imagined they were racing in the Indianapolis 500? Boy, I hope a police officer isn't reading this.

License to Party

By now you can see I don't do e-mail invitations. It's hard to, when there are such fun and inventive ways to invite people to your shindig. For a NASCAR party, pick up some inexpensive plastic license plate holders at an auto supply store. Print a clever vanity plate like "UR INVTD" onto a standard sheet of paper, trim it to fit the holder, and tape it on the back. The back of the license can list the specific details.

Flag Wall

You know I love wall treatments. This super-easy racing flag decoration consists of ten-inch squares of foam core alternating in black and white. I didn't even cut the squares; ask your local art supply store if they will trim your foam core for a small fee. It's worth it. The squares are applied to the wall with small dabs of poster putty for easy removal.

Funnel Clouds

Like I said, I'm never going to change the oil in my car myself. So what do I do with all these oil funnels I bought? I know, make them into bud vases. Just hide a small cup underneath the funnel to store the water. I put big China mums in the funnels because they look like billowing clouds. When placed inside the track, they look like cumulous clouds over the race.

Racetrack Table

Okay, this takes me back to my Hot Wheel days. If you have a buffet table, or even if you're planning a sit-down dinner, place a toy racetrack around the perimeter of the table. The track dramatically frames your food and decorations, so your guests will race to the table.

Dining Hub

Guests will be rubbernecking when they see these hubcaps used as serving platters. I bought a set of four used hubcaps on eBay for $7.99. After washing them thoroughly with soap and water to remove all the brake dust, I gave them one final cleansing in the dishwasher so they'd be food-safe. When the hubcap's upside down, it holds snacks. Turn it the other way, and you can place a bowl of dip in the center.

Checkered Flag Toothpicks

You really can't have too many checkered flags at this party. Turn regular toothpicks into flags by gluing some checkered paper around the tip of the toothpicks. I created the checkered paper myself on the computer, cut it into rectangles, and adhered the pieces to the toothpicks with a glue stick.

Party Tip

When you're hosting a party, there's always the question of where to store everyone's coats. I recommend placing a shower curtain tension rod in the hallway to make a temporary clothes rack. The added benefit of a clothes rack in the middle of the hallway is that it acts as a subtle barrier to the bedrooms, in case you don't want people venturing into your private sanctuary.

CHAPTER 15

Spy Summit

A Rendezvous of Secret Agents

Who hasn't fantasized about being an international secret agent like James Bond or Emma Peele? I certainly have. It is the ultimate glamor job. Jet-setting around the world, playing with cool gadgets, spending other people's money, and fighting diabolical megalomaniacs—come to think of it, that sounds like my job as an interior designer. The name's Fong. Jonathan Fong. Secret Asian Man.

With this spy party, you'll be entertaining friends while you save the world. Not a bad way to spend the evening. I've envisioned an underground fortress in Antarctica where you, our hero, are meeting your fellow operatives, one of whom is a double agent and possibly your evil arch nemesis in disguise. Above the table floats a world map highlighting the coordinates of various secret headquarters. The world's fate hangs in the balance as you sip on martinis with fluorescent ice cubes. You keep one eye on the deadly tarantula, just inches away. And as you rest your drink on the fur-lined table, you have one thought: "Is it time to take the chicken fingers out of the oven yet?" Oh, the life of a superspy. Or is that a superhost?

Top Secret

Back in the days of the TV series *Mission: Impossible,* the superagent Jim Phelps received instructions on tapes that would self-destruct. It's the modern world now, so design your invitation on the computer, convert it to a JPEG or a PDF file, and burn it onto a compact disc. Then design a cover for the CD case that tells the recipient that the contents are top secret. It will certainly pique his or her interest.

A WORD ABOUT THE TABLE DECOR

I wanted to draw your attention to some of the items I used to dress the table for this secret-agent party. In the photo on page 126, the geodesic dome is actually a lamp from Ikea that I had trouble putting together. I just gave up, and what was left was a sphere. I thought it looked appropriately space-age under the map of the world. I've also scattered sheepskin rugs all over the table to give a sense that we're underground in Antarctica. *Brrr . . .* it's cold down here. The blue light sculptures sitting on top of the tarantula and scorpion vases are light fixtures from Ikea as well, except there was no assembly required. I liked their futuristic bearing.

Tarantula Under Glass

Danger is always present when you're a secret agent. Villains seem to enjoy hiding tarantulas and scorpions in your bed at night. But you're not afraid. You caught this tarantula with your bare hands and placed it under glass to show that you laugh in the face of danger. Ha!

Sorry, I got a little carried away. What you see is a rubber tarantula under an upside-down vase. There's also a rubber scorpion elsewhere on the table. They make sinister, but fun, table accents.

World Map Coordinates

In spy movies, there is always a big map of the world hovering above the conference tables of world leaders, military generals, agents, and villains. In the more high-tech headquarters, the map is sometimes a hologram that floats by itself. I recreated a "map of world domination" by placing a world map on a clear piece of plastic. It's the lights that give it the dramatic impact.

WHAT YOU'LL NEED
1 thin, 2- x 3-feet (approx.) piece of plastic
Scissors
1 world map
Spray adhesive
Drill
Fishing line
3M Cord Clips
At least 5 Floralytes
Poster putty

1   Purchase a thin piece of plastic at an art supply store or a plastics warehouse. Trim it with scissors to about 2 x 3 feet.

2   Cut a world map out of an atlas. Apply some spray glue to the map side and adhere it to the plastic.

3   Drill a hole in the two top corners of the plastic sheet.

4   Hang the plastic from the ceiling with fishing line, hooking it onto 3M Cord Clips.

5   Now the fun part. Purchase portable lights, called Floralytes, to stick onto the map. They are about the size of a tea light, come in different colors, light up with a twist, and will stay lit for twenty-four hours. Stick them on various coordinates of the map with a dab of poster putty.

Mod Wall Treatment

This wall treatment is so James Bond. In my book *Walls that Wow,* I featured another style of cardboard wall tiles made by the same company, MIO. The 12- x 12-inch tiles pictured here, called Flow, come in a variety of colors, and they're attached to the wall with double-sided tape. They make a dramatic backdrop for a table or a piece of furniture. It's also good to know that these tiles are made from 100 percent post- and pre-consumer waste paper. I also have a suspicion that if you touch the wall in just the right place, it will swivel to reveal a secret scientific research laboratory.

Gold Fingers

Now to my favorite idea in the whole book—which shows how twisted I am. To recreate the famous scene from the movie *Goldfinger,* I spray-painted a fashion doll metallic-gold and placed her on a platter of chicken fingers. To achieve the flawless gold effect, I first covered the doll's hair with masking tape and then sprayed on a layer of primer before painting her gold. As the song goes, "Gold Fingers. They're the snack, the snack with the Midas touch." Can you tell I used to work in advertising?

Party Tip

Plan for three glasses and four cocktail napkins per guest. Guests should have a fresh glass before you change their wine. Yes, I know glasses usually go on the right, but in this book I sometimes put them on the left, because rules like that take the fun out of parties.

Laser Ice Cubes

I found these plastic ice cubes at a party supply store. They can be submerged in your cocktail and have three light settings: fast blink, slow blink, and continuous light. They're something Dr. Evil would enjoy . . . for one *million* dollars!

CHAPTER 16

Girls' Night In

It's All about You

The women in my life are busy. They spend every day running errands for family members when they're not working, and they rarely have down-time for themselves. A few years ago my two sisters visited me for a weekend getaway, and it was the first time they had been away from their husbands and kids in over a decade. It was hard to fathom, but I guess this is not uncommon. So this Girl's Night In party is my gift to all the ladies out there who need a little break from their daily routines. Please know that if I could reach out through these pages and rub your feet, I would.

I also love the ideas in this chapter because I'm a big fan of spa nights. Apply gunk to my face, unclog my pores, feed me chocolate, and I'm a happy camper. So I tell you what, men, you can have a guy's night in party like this, too. Just leave a few beer bottles and pizza boxes around the next day so no one gets suspicious. We all deserve to be pampered now and then, don't we?

Soap Talk

Imagine the reaction when your girl-friends go to wash their faces and find soap bars with their faces printed on them. The best part about these per-sonalized soap bars is that the image won't wash off. It's sealed in.

WHAT YOU'LL NEED FOR ONE BAR

Photograph of guest
1 bar soap (pictured is
    Neutrogena Glycerin Soap)
Scissors
Foam brush
Mod Podge
Aluminum tin tray
Sauté pan that's larger than
    the aluminum tray
Beeswax pellets
Tongs

NOTE: Be extra careful when doing this project, because you'll be working with boil-ing water and hot wax. Never let a child near this project without adult supervision.

1 Using your computer, size the photograph to the same dimensions as the soap bar. Print the image and trim it.

2 When selecting soap, purchase bar(s) that have flat sides; otherwise, it will be hard to adhere the image to a soap bar with a rounded surface. Using a foam brush, adhere the image to the soap bar with Mod Podge, which is an all-in-one glue and sealer that is used for decoupage projects. Then paint a layer of Mod Podge over the image and let it dry.

3 Create a shallow double boiler by placing an aluminum tin tray inside a larger sauté pan. Fill the sauté pan with about a quarter- to half-inch layer of water. Then place a small amount of beeswax pellets, which are used in candle making, in the aluminum tin. There should be about a quarter-inch layer of wax pellets in the tin. The weight of the wax pellets should keep the aluminum tin from floating on the water in the sauté pan. Heat the water in the pan until the wax melts.

4 Grab the soap bar facedown with a pair of tongs. I use two hands for a better grip. With the tongs, dip the soap bar in the melted wax to seal the image. It takes a little wrist finesse to dip the soap in the wax so that you only have a thin, smooth layer of wax. Two tips to help you: (1) Be really fast. The slower you are, the more wax will build up on the soap. (2) Do not dunk the soap straight down into the wax, as it will cause air pockets and an uneven finish. The key is to dip the wax in a pendulum motion. The diagram bottom left depicts the angle in which the soap bar should skim the wax. Finally, never dip the soap twice, or the wax will be so thick you won't see the image.

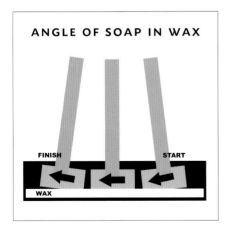

ANGLE OF SOAP IN WAX

FINISH   START

WAX

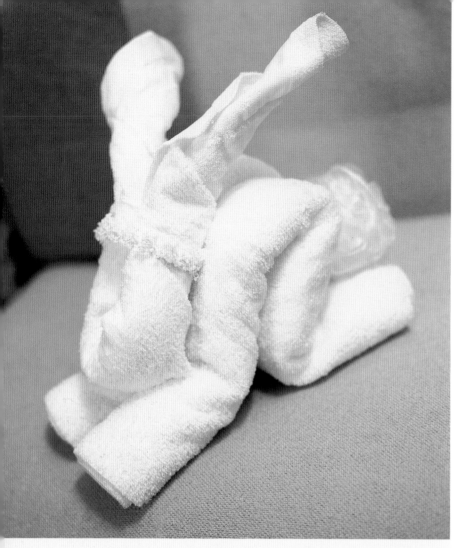

Towel Bunnies

How fun it will be for each guest to have a bunny, made of towels, waiting for her. I've chosen white towels, but you can use any color you like. After you learn this project, you will never stay at a hotel again without transforming all the bathroom towels into animals.

WHAT YOU'LL NEED FOR ONE BUNNY
1 bath towel
1 hand towel
2 washcloths
1 scrunchie
1 mesh sponge

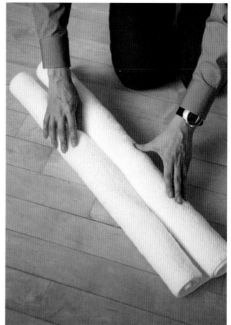

1 Lay out your bath towel. Roll the two ends lengthwise until they meet in the middle. It should look like two long tubes side by side.

2 Bend the towel as shown to form the bunny's legs and body.

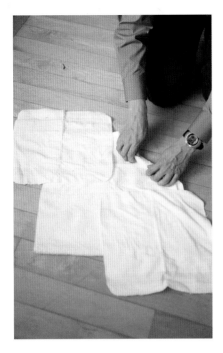

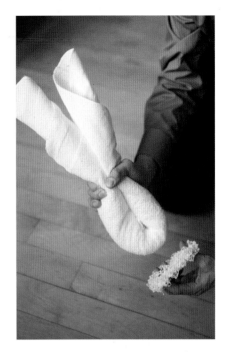

3 To make the head and ears, start with the hand towel and fold it once to create a square. Then place two washcloths at opposite corners of the square. It will look like three overlapping squares in a diagonal, with the middle square larger than the other two.

4 Starting with the corner of the hand towel in the middle, roll the towel. When you reach the smaller washcloths, incorporate them into your roll. What you will end up with is one long tube with two pointy ends.

5 Fold the tube in half, slide a scrunchie a third of the way down, and you've formed the head and the ears. Rest the head on top of the body. Finally, place a mesh sponge on the bunny's behind to form the tail.

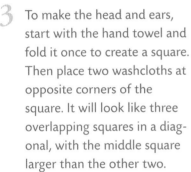

TOP 10 CHICK FLICKS

Girls' night wouldn't be complete without a chick flick marathon. Here are my favorites:

13 Going on 30
Sense and Sensibility
Bridget Jones's Diary
Kate & Leopold
While You Were Sleeping
Ever After
The First Wives Club
My Big Fat Greek Wedding
The Devil Wears Prada
Notting Hill

Flip-Flopped

Provide flip-flops that have been decorated with rhinestones and silk flowers for your friends to lounge in. It would be even more fun to break out a bag of rhinestones along with a hot glue gun and let all the girls decorate their own.

Croquembouche

Of course, you can't have a girls' night without a decadent dessert. This croquembouche is great for parties, because you can all sit around and pick cream puffs off the "tree" between scintillating tidbits of gossip. I use store-bought chocolate-covered cream puffs from the frozen food aisle.

1   Purchase a Styrofoam cone from the craft store, insert toothpicks into the foam, and then stick the cream puffs onto the toothpicks. The presentation is so stylish. However, when I make this dessert, I end up eating a lot more cream puffs out of the box than those that get displayed.

Party Tip

Consider hiring a masseuse with a portable massage chair to give everyone a back and neck massage. Don't tell your guests ahead of time; let it be a surprise.

CHAPTER 17

Best Western

A Roundup for Urban Cowboys

I'll always remember the first time I went horseback riding. I begged my parents for the $5 to join my church group for the afternoon outing. I was assigned the gentlest horse, named Willow, and excitedly made my way along the trail. Willow was on autopilot, so I didn't really have to do much in terms of steering or stopping. Still, I was thrilled because I was imagining myself as one of the Cartwright brothers on *Bonanza*, or at least their Chinese servant Hop Sing. Halfway through the ride, however, I started to itch. Uncontrollably. When I finally got off my horse and looked in the mirror, I saw that I was covered with hives. Nice way to find out I was allergic to horses.

Oh well, being a cowboy was not in my cards. Now the closest I get to a rodeo is Rodeo Drive. But that doesn't mean I don't like to kick up a little hypoallergenic dust with my boots now and then and go honky-tonking. Western parties are fun for everyone, because they're casual, and even a little bit raucous. The one goal for everyone is to have a rip-roaring good time. So round up your friends and tell them to giddy on over, but to leave their horses at home.

Hay There

It's easy to make hay. (Is there a pun there?) Start with a small box (I used a clear acrylic one), and place your invitation inside. Then take strands of raffia and wrap it around and around the box. Compact the raffia tightly, and every now and then, tie it down with some string to keep it in place. Keep going until the box is completely covered.

You now have a bale of hay with a hidden message inside, kind of like a cowboy fortune cookie.

Saddle Barstool

My neighbors found an old saddle at a garage sale, so I asked to borrow it for this Western party. The saddle sits right on top of a standard stool to make a mechanical bull. All right, it's not mechanical at all, but all your friends can pretend it is. They'll be lining up to get their pictures taken on it—I promise.

Cowboy Boot Centerpieces

Everyone will get a kick out of these colorful centerpieces. One of your friends surely has a pair of cowboy boots you can borrow, or you can find a pair at a thrift store. Fill a cylindrical vase with water or floral foam, slide the vase into the boot, and load the boot up with flowers.

Bandana Markers

The only thing worse than sipping warm beer (or, in my case, warm root beer) is accidentally taking a swig of someone else's. But that won't be a problem if you assign color-coded bandanas to tie around everyone's bottles. They're certainly more rugged than dainty wine charms.

Hat Skewers

When I was in Fort Worth, I went to a Western store and tried on every cowboy hat in the place, but they all made me look like I had a pinhead. I have better luck using cowboy hats as serving platters. Select a hat that will stand on its own, and place some heavy rocks inside so that it doesn't tip. Then cut some floral foam to fit inside the hat and cover the floral foam with some shredded lettuce. Now you can stick skewers into the hat.

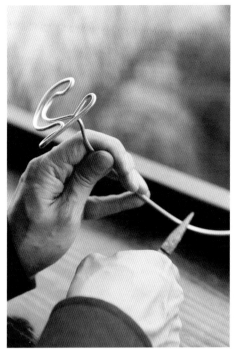

1 All you have to do is twist the wire, bending it into the desired initial with a pair of pliers. The bamboo handle at the end is strictly decorative, since you wouldn't actually put this branding iron in the fire. I use my iron as a paperweight or as a head scratcher when I'm feeling contemplative.

Party Tip

Allow four to six hors d'oeuvres per person if you're serving a full meal afterward. If it's just an hors d'oeuvres party, you should provide eight to ten per person. Large platters of cheese and crudités are great ways to supplement the hors d'oeuvres.

Branding Iron

Here's a fun way to usher your guests out the door: Brand them. Actually, these aren't real branding irons, but they are fun party favors. My friend Monica Heeren of Two Crafty Ladies showed me how to make branding irons out of armature wire, which is sold in art supply stores for sculpting. It's very lightweight and pliable.

CHAPTER 18

Broadway's Bark Mitzvah

A Party That Goes to the Dogs

My trusty canine companion, Broadway, is a member of the family. She's included in all holiday celebrations, and she always gets a little birthday party to commemorate the day I adopted her. But when she grew up from puppyhood to adulthood, she deserved a special party. That's when she had her bark mitzvah. Now, I've been to a lot of bar mitzvahs and bat mitzvahs, so I know the drill. The young adult reads from the Torah, he or she gets presents, and everyone eats. Broadway loves to eat and get presents, so it was just a matter of teaching her the Torah. Everything came out sounding like the same bark, but since I don't speak Hebrew, this proud parent was still impressed.

Dog parties are all the rage, not because we've gone overboard in anthropomorphizing our pets, but because we are constantly looking for ways to show our loyal four-legged friends our love. It's really the least we can do for all that they do for us. When you're planning a dog party, you have to keep two audiences in mind: the dogs and their crazy humans. And it's usually the humans who are the most trouble to wrangle. Oy.

Come! Stay!

LEONARD

is invited to
Broadway's Bark Mitzvah.
August 26th,
4:00 in the afternoon
at Broadway's house.
B.Y.O.B.
(Bring your own bone.)

Playing Tag

When sending invitations, personalize the invitations with dog tags engraved with your friends' names. Most local pet supply stores have a self-service pet tag machine that engraves while you wait. Encourage your friends to wear their tags at the party. They sure beat those "Hi, my name is _____" name-tag stickers.

Party Tip

The dog toys shown in these pages were generously provided by The Modern Dog, a delightful shopping emporium and utopia for dog lovers, that is located in Venice, California. The Modern Dog's proprietors, Guy Miracle and Lance Castro, offer these helpful hints when throwing a dog party of your own:

- If you are going to have birthday cake, make sure the pieces are individually cut before giving them to the dogs. Or, better yet, use doggie cupcakes. This will cut down on potential dog conflicts.
- Make sure to give your gift bags or toys near the end of the party, or as the guests are leaving. This will also help to reduce any squabbling.
- Remember, while this might be a dog party, it is also an excellent opportunity to build relationships with other pet owners. Make it for the humans as well.
- Accidents happen, so be prepared. Keep plenty of clean-up aides handy. There is always one guest who can't hold his treats!
- Pets enjoy entertainment, too. Consider hiring an obedience trainer, or, better yet, a pet psychic or pet photographer. This is fun for everyone and will create a memorable occasion.
- Make sure you have plenty of space for your guests. Plan to have your party at your favorite dog park, backyard, or doggie day-care center.

Chocolate Chip Bones

Remember, at this bark mitzvah, you're feeding two audiences: the dogs and their human guardians. A little bit of role reversal is fun here, so the people food will look like it's for the dogs, and the dogs' food will look like people food. One idea is to make chocolate chip cookies in the shape of bones for your human guests. I used a bone-shaped cookie cutter with pre-made cookie dough. Here's a hint: When these cookies bake, they may spread and lose their bone shape, so press the cookie cutter on them again when they're warm right out of the oven. You'll want to keep these cookies out of the reach of dogs, *especially* if you've used chocolate chips. Chocolate contains theobromine, a chemical that is toxic to dogs.

Floral Fire Hydrant

Of all the beautiful floral arrangements I've ever made, this floral fire hydrant is Broadway's favorite.

WHAT YOU'LL NEED
2 bricks of floral foam
Steak knife
100 (approx.) red carnations
2 red plastic cups
2 red interlocking plastic plates

1 Cut the floral foam bricks in half so that you have four pieces in total. Carve three of the pieces into foam cylinders by rounding out the corners. Carve the fourth piece so that it is a dome. Soak the floral foam in water.

2 Making the fire hydrant is very much like making the floral cakes in my book *Flowers that Wow*. Snip the red carnations, leaving about an inch of stem. Take one of the foam cylinders and begin inserting the carnation stems around the circumference of the foam. Start at the bottom of the cylinder and complete one row of carnations before moving up to the next row. You can fit around twelve to fifteen carnations per layer, depending on how big they are. You only need two rows to cover the foam cylinder. Once you've made one, repeat for the second cylinder. Stack the second cylinder on top of the first one.

3 Before inserting carnations into the third foam cylinder, wedge two red plastic cups on opposite sides of the foam. These will be the valves of the fire hydrant. Fill in the rest of the foam with carnations and stack this section on top of the first two.

4 You're now left with a dome-shaped piece of floral foam. Insert the red carnations to cover the foam. Place the dome on top of two interlocking red plastic plates. Then stack the layer onto the first three.

Paw Print Floor Decals

Lead your guests to the outdoor party area with this trail of dog prints. You can have removable vinyl floor decals made at your local sign shop. They rub onto the floor and are easy to peel off when the party is over. Be sure the sign shop puts a coating on them especially designed for floor decals to give them more traction. Just draw your own set of paws and have them print you a dozen or so.

Favorite Dishes

Here's another fun role-reversal idea. Serve all the people snacks in dog dishes. Be sure to have the dishes up on tables so that the dogs—and people—don't get confused.

Haute Dog

I'm pretty sure discriminating dogs notice when you've put a little extra effort in the food presentation. This vertical stack of wet and dry dog food looks like a culinary masterpiece. Make sure your human guests don't think it's for them.

1 Purchase a cylindrical food mold from a restaurant supply store, or just use an empty soup can with both top and bottom lids removed. Spray the inside of the mold with a vegetable oil release spray.

2 Work on a piece of parchment first, rather than the actual plate. Spoon alternating layers of wet and dry dog food into the mold. If you have different colors of wet food, that's even better.

3 Slowly remove the mold over a plate. Lean a few dog treats on the food stack to give the presentation more height. To top it all off with a flourish, drizzle some dog gravy onto the plate.

Resource Directory

Bon Soirée (pages 16–23)
French postcards:
eBay (wwwebay.com)

French sparkling lemonade:
Bay Cities Italian Deli
1517 Lincoln Blvd.
Santa Monica, CA
90401
310-395-1575
(www.baycitiesitaliandeli.com)

Sofa duvet cover:
Ikea (www.ikea.com)

Zen Fusion (pages 24–31)
Bamboo poles and sheet moss:
Moskatel's
738 S. Wall St.
Los Angeles, CA 90014
213-689-4590

Metal bins:
Ikea (www.ikea.com)

Chopsticks:
Cost Plus World Market

Chicken skewers and shrimp tempura:
Costco (www.costco.com)

Stamps used for fan invitation:
Small Flower: Magenta
(www.magentastyle.com)

Dragonfly, Butterfly with Ferns: Hero Arts
(www.heroarts.com)

"House of Lotus Collection": Oxford
Impressions (www.oxfordimpressions.com)

Round Lantern, Small: A Stamp in the
Hand Co. (www.astampinthehand.com)

Asian Image, Woman with Hat:
Inkadinkado
(www.inkadinkado.com)

Wisteria, Butterfly, Hanabishi: Mari & Me,
(www.mariandme.com)

Bird with flower: Viva Las Vegastamps!
(www.vivalasvegastamps.com)

One Night in Morocco (pages 32–41)
Spices:
India Sweets and Spices
9409 Venice Blvd.
Culver City, CA 90232
310-837-5286

Floral mesh:
Moskatel's
738 S. Wall St.
Los Angeles, CA 90014
213-689-4590

Rock Like an Egyptian (pages 42–49)
Stone platters:
Home Depot (www.homedepot.com)

Betty Crocker Drizzlers:
At your local supermarket

Pyramid food mold:
Surfas Restaurant and Supply
8824 National Blvd.
Culver City, CA 90232
866-799-4770
(www.surfasonline.com)

Jane Austen Picnic (pages 50–59)
Avery Dark T-Shirt Transfers:
Staples (www.staples.com)

Floral foam bouquet holders:
(www.afloral.com)

Lazertran Waterslide Decal Paper:
Dick Blick Art Materials
(www.dickblick.com)

Stamp for altered book:
"Time for Tea": Simply Stamped
(www.simplystamped.com)

Winter Wonderland (pages 62–69)
Snow globes:
Michael's (www.michaels.com)

Snow powder:
Cart Planet, Inc.
818-501-2036
(www.snow-powder.com)

3M Cord Clips with Command Adhesive:
Staples (www.staples.com)

It's Easy Being Green (pages 70–75)
Bamboo plates:
Koontz Hardware
8914 Santa Monica Blvd.
West Hollywood, CA 90069
310-652-0123
(www.koontzhardware.com)

Wheat grass:
Whole Foods (www.wholefoods.com)

Recycling center information:
(www.earth911.org)

¡Viva the Party! (pages 76–81)
Piñatas:
Your local party supply store

Chili pepper light covers:
(www.gidyup.com)

Starfish and Stripes (pages 82–87)
Seashells:
Thai Teak
2400 Main Street
Santa Monica, CA 90405
310-581-4255

Shell bowls:
Surfas Restaurant and Supply
8824 National Blvd.
Culver City, CA 90232
866-799-4770
(www.surfasonline.com)

Think Pink (pages 88–95)
Place mats:
Linens 'n Things (www.lnt.com)

Ball chain key chains
(www.ballchain.com)

Silk rose petals, feather boas:
Your local crafts store

Pre-made fondant:
Surfas Restaurant and Supply
8824 National Blvd.
Culver City, CA 90232
866-799-4770
(www.surfasonline.com)

Stamps for invitation:
Floral Background: Savvy Stamps
(www.savvystamps.com)

"Celebrate," "Life": Rubberstamp Ave.
(www.rubberstampave.com)

Spellbound (pages 96–103)
Spoon bending information:
(www.jackhouck.com)

Invisible ink pens:
Circuit City
(www.circuitcity.com)

Breakfast at Jonathan's (pages 106–113)
Velvet jewelry boxes:
(www.jewelrysupply.com)

Mirrored jewelry box:
Target (www.target.com)

Embroidery hoops:
Your local crafts and sewing arts store

Faucet handles:
Home Depot (www.homedepot.com)

Come to the Cabaret (pages 114–119)
Napkin stamp:
Staples (www.staples.com)

Shower curtain tension rod:
Bed, Bath & Beyond
(www.bedbathandbeyond.com)
Decorator round tables, rope lights:
Target (www.target.com)

Vroom to Party (pages 120–125)
License plate holders:
Kragen Auto Parts
(www.kragen.com)

Hubcaps:
eBay (www.ebay.com)

Racetrack:
Toys 'r' Us (www.toysrus.com)

Spy Summit (pages 126–133)
Plastic sheet:
Plastic Mart
11600 Pico Blvd.
W. Los Angeles, CA 90064
310-268-1404
(www.plasticmart.net)

Flow wall tiles:
MIO
340 North 12th Street Unit 301
Philadelphia, PA 19107
215-925-9359
(www.mioculture.com)

Tarantula and scorpion:
Store for Knowledge
(www.storeforknowledge.com)

Floralytes and Lite Cubes:
(www.partylytes.com)

Girl's Night In (pages 134–143)
Hershey's Symphony Bars:
At your local supermarket or in volume at:
(www.itsalldirect2u.com)

Cream puffs:
Smart and Final

Best Western (pages 144–149)
Armature Wire:
Mittel's Art Center
2016 Lincoln Blvd.
Santa Monica, CA 90405
310-399-9500

Broadway's Bark Mitzvah (pages 150–157)
Dog toys:
The Modern Dog
1611 Abbot Kinney Blvd.
Venice, CA 90291
310-450-BARK
(www.come-sit-stay.com)

Additional Resources
Supplies for the invitations made by the
Card Club Ladies:
Stampin' From the Heart
Karen Hutchinson, Proprietor
11720 Washington Place
Los Angeles, CA 90066

Food Stylist/Chef
Amy Jurist
Amy's Culinary Adventures
www.amysculinaryadventures.com
818-761-6716

Additional supplies from:
The Cat's Pajamas Rubber Stamps
Alma De La Rosa, Proprietor
1519-39th Avenue
San Francisco, CA 94122-3015

Index